NEW PASSIVE INCOME

Converting Opportunities into
Stacks of Cash

A. T. JAMES

ISBN: 9798637840717

ACKNOWLEDGMENTS

I would like to acknowledge all those that helped with the penning of this book. I had many ideas that needed to be refined before including them within the confines of these pages, so I thank those that helped refine and reshape my ideas.

I would also like to thank you, the reader, for showing interest in this book. I hope it provides a semblance of ideas that you can use to create streams of passive income.

TABLE OF CONTENTS

<u>PREFACE</u>

LEGAL DISCLAIMER

You, the reader, are 100% responsible for what you do with the information in this book. Even though I discuss activities that, performed in specific manners, might be against set rules or illegal, I do not condone or suggest any behavior or activity that could be construed as illegal in the eyes of the laws and rules of any governing body.

Before you delve into this book, understand that many of the ideas and list items discussed may or may not be completely legal given the area in which you live or the scale at which you operate.

Some list items might remain as part-time, under-the-table gigs, or they might stem into full, large scale business ideas that might require registering your passive income revenue stream as a business and paying taxes. Different cities, counties, regions, or even countries have varying laws that might directly relate to the passive income stream that you develop.

There is something to be said about plausible deniability and strategic ignorance, but in the true nature of these concepts, I won't mention them here, for obvious reasons. If you start asking questions about different policies or rules, the answers you receive might not be the answers you want to hear. With that said, you may want to consider the legal or obligatory ramifications of "bending" laws and rules (or county codes, city ordinances, etc.). The consequences of bending these "legal guidelines" may be immediate, or they may never occur. Will the IRS care if you made an extra few hundred bucks by selling things on Craigslist? Maybe not. Will the IRS care if you are pulling in $20,000 a year from social media influencing? Probably. However, some social media influencers might collect that $20,000 and *never* report it to the IRS. It all depends on the level of risk, or amount of consequences, you might or might not want to face.

The amount of risk or consequence that you want to face is completely up to you.

I am not saying that generating passive income is illegal, and most of the ideas I present in this book are completely legal. However, it is important to note that the vast majority of passive income opportunities can be utilized on the legal level as well as the illegal level, and the line between legal and illegal is not always evident. For instance, I discuss boarding horses. Depending on where you board the horses, the legalities of doing so might depend on the amount of horses you board, the zoning of your land, possible city or county ordinances against having "livestock", or even how much land each horse has access to. Let's go a step further and build a shade structure/stable for the horses you board. Again, the line between legal and illegal could be drawn by permits, easements, the size of the structure, or even whether the structure is permanent or temporary.

Keep in mind that there are plenty of governing boards or agencies that make and enforce a variety of rules. If you care to follow the absolute letter of the law, be sure to check all applicable governing systems which might include:

Federal law
State law
Regional law
County ordinances
City ordinances
Township rules
Company policy
Home Owner Association policy

You may want to make sure you understand where that line is and if, or when, you cross it. Or maybe not. Remember what I said about plausible deniability and strategic ignorance.

While this is a legal disclaimer, I am not a lawyer, so the only real advice I can offer is to consult a lawyer if you feel like you need to.

ETHICAL DISCLAIMER

While most laws are pretty straight forward, one area that is particularly sticky centers on personal ethics. While some might feel validated in whatever they do despite other's opinions, keep in mind that when it comes to many passive income streams, there might be some questions or concerns about personal ethics.

The majority of the list items I discuss are honest and do not go against the ethical norms society has helped construct, but the line between what is good practice versus unethical practice is very blurry.

Even though the spectrum of ethics is as broad as it is vague, there are some very obvious ethical dilemmas that might pop up as you start your passive income revenue streams. When we get further into the list, some of these will become wildly apparent, but for now, some basic issues might involve the idea of moonlighting, bending an employer's policy, or reusing items or supplies meant for other clients. While these might seem somewhat innocent, they could quickly become complicated ethical dilemmas.

As an example, is it really okay to sublet a room? A clause stating the specifics of this might be in a rental agreement, but what if the original renter never checks, or doesn't bother to ask? Aside from possibly going against the original rental agreement, even if subletting was alright, the property owner might want to know that a room is being subletted. These kinds of issues might develop when a friend visits, and that visit turns into a more long term stay. Maybe in this instance, the original renter did not think about subletting the room, even as a passive income stream, but now he is asking his friend to help cover some of the rent for the next month. Since there was no exact "move-in date" the ethics of this type of situation become that much muddier. When should the original renter let the property owner know? Should they even worry about it if the friend isn't planning on staying? How long does a casual visit really last before it turns into something more serious and more ethically questionable?

Let's use the idea of education and cheating as another example. Obviously cheating is unethical, as this has been hammered into our heads for years. However, this long held ethical standard gets pretty murky when you ask different people what cheating means to them.

> Is it cheating to copy off of someone else's test? What about their homework? What if it was a "group assignment"?

> In an open book test, especially in modern times where many textbooks are digital, is using the Find function cheating?

> In a group project, is delegation cheating, or should each group member work on each task together?

If allowed to use a notecard on an exam, is it cheating to use a computer to print out a smaller font on the notecard than your handwriting would be?

Is it cheating to share test answers with classmates after a test? What if other students that have yet to take the test might be listening?

Would it be cheating to purchase the instructor's version of the text?

Would it be cheating to use your friend's notes to study for a test?

Is it cheating to post previous responses to case studies, homework questions, or other assignments on user-based websites? What about after you graduate? What about after that particular class's professor retires?

Would it be unethical to act as a private tutor for specific classes?

I pose these questions not only to show a spectrum of personal ethics and morals pertaining to cheating, but to also introduce the concept of situational ethics. In most of these cases, the opinions of students, graduates, teachers, or seasoned professionals would vary greatly from question to question. I remember a specific professor allowing students to use internet searches if they took notes on their laptop or tablet in class, but if a student only used paper notes, they weren't afforded the same luxury, even though it was in the same class! Undoubtedly, some would give different examples of when a particular activity might be considered cheating and when it might be considered ethical or even a standard practice.

In all reality, I am writing this ethical disclaimer to:

1. Absolve myself from any questions of moral turpitude. Even though I am writing about potentially unethical practices, these writings do not represent my own ethical ideas and/or my personal moral compass.

2. Give myself some credibility. I am not writing this book with the intention that the reader will bend the ethical or moral standpoints of themselves and their social groups. Although I discuss some ideas throughout this book, there are numerous list items I have included that go against my own ethics and morals. I have included these in an effort to be all-inclusive, and to respect those with varying ethics.

3. Give perspective. Even the most well-intended activities can be seen as unethical from another person's viewpoint. Also, the path from ethical to unethical is a slippery slope. The more you dive into

unethical behavior, the more likely you are to eventually find yourself sliding further and further.

When it comes to ethics, my best advice is that you develop your own code of conduct that you adhere to as best you can. It is up to you to draw the line and set the boundaries needed to sleep peacefully at night. Again, the majority of the list items I discuss are honest and do not go against the ethical normalcies society has helped construct.

PART 1
Before You Quit Your Day Job

INTRODUCTION

Have you ever found yourself dreamily looking out your office window, debating if your hourly wage is actually worth the hours, minutes, even seconds, of your life ticking by? Are you tired of spending your precious time making measly sums of money just to pad someone else's wallet? Do you want to live a lifestyle where there are no bosses, supervisors, deadlines, meetings, or other engagements that pull you away from what you really want to do? Do you love your job but want to boost your income beyond your salary or hourly wage? Do you want to make more per hour but retain the same responsibilities? Do you want to turn that expensive hobby into a money maker?

Let me introduce you to new passive income.

Passive income used to be somewhat of an exclusive secret. You might picture investors living off of the interest of their investments, doing virtually anything they want without a care in the world. While this might be a kind of Holy Grail for passive income earners, this type of investing might require a substantial amount of capital, and it certainly comes with more risk than is ever advertised. In truth, there are countless opportunities to earn passive income that require little to no upfront costs.

Through this book, I not only hope to educate you, but also proffer up solid ideas that will help make your dream lifestyle a reality. If you want to make money while you sleep and never worry about deadlines, conference calls, or rush hour ever again, this book will give you the information and ideas you need to achieve those goals.

BEFORE YOU QUIT YOUR DAY JOB

Google "get rich quick" and you will be sure to come across pages and pages of different passive income (labeled as PI from this point on) schemes that spokespersons, entertainers, entrepreneurs, and business leaders alike will claim to work with little to no risk. Some of these schemes may be sold as having massive, instant returns. Some of these schemes may even require payment to special groups to not only get started, but to also advance to higher tiers with the promise of exponential increases to PI. For that reason, I find myself obligated to help weed out those types of PI streams that are not necessarily beneficial, or are outright scams. Every PI stream and opportunity should follow some basic business principles, and understanding these principles will help you determine the lucrative opportunities to take part in, as well as the pitfalls to avoid. The business principles that relate directly to PI are easy to understand and include value, the cost of making money, and time involvement.

Value

The first business principle that relates to PI is the idea of value. Consumers purchase goods and services based on the value that they feel they are receiving for their money. Businesses and companies pay employees because they find value in the contributions of employees. An extremely simple, yet accurate depiction of value comes from the old saying "follow the money". Even without considering PI, this concept is straightforward as a basic idea of trading goods for a perceived value.

For instance, a person with no accounting experience applying to work at an accounting firm will not be seen as a valuable contribution to the firm, and may instead get a job in the mailroom for an hourly rate. On the opposite side of the scenario, an accountant with decades of experience applying to the same firm may be offered their own office and a salary-based pay. The firm sees the value of the first applicant as very low, whereas the second applicant may be highly valued by the firm. This is simply because the person with experience can help to increase the revenues of the firm. The applicant that winds up in the mailroom might be extremely good at sorting mail, but the firm does not value that specific activity as much as the activities of a seasoned accountant.

When it comes to consumer goods, the idea of value gets a little more skewed. As an example, a car's value is extremely relative. For instance, a truck may have differing values from car buyer to car buyer. A rancher that needs to use the truck on their ranch would see a high value in the truck, whereas a person looking for a commuter car might not even consider the truck as an option. When it comes to used trucks, it gets even trickier, as some buyers might see basic maintenance as an expected part of the product; some sellers use terms like "well maintained" to add perceived value to the truck they are selling. In both of these examples it is important to remember that the truck remains the same, but the perceived value changes as different shoppers assign different values to the product.

Value can be added, accumulated, or derived from a product, but when dealing with PI, it is important to consider what aspect of the PI function is actually valuable. The value of email affiliates comes from more people clicking through to the web store and making a purchase. The value of a sponsorship or paid promotion is branding with the intent of a brand becoming more well-known. In essence, the question that must be asked is "why would someone pay for this service?" or "why would they pay me to do that?". If that answer is unclear, chances are high that the get-rich-quick scheme is simply just a scheme. If there is a real value, it should be obvious.

While this is just a quick glimpse at some value functions of PI, this shows how there is a real substance to some of the different offerings of PI activities. Of course, these will be described in greater detail later on.

Some examples of PI as it relates to value are:

PI Function	→	Perceived Value
Real estate rentals	→	Renter does not have to purchase a home
Flipping real estate	→	Added value to a home or land
Selling used cars	→	Buyer may not qualify for a car loan, could be a good deal for the buyer
Affiliated links	→	Webstore generates sales from your audience through you
Selling an eBook	→	People pay for knowledge they might gain from the eBook

Sponsored content	→	Company uses your content to increase their brand recognition
Selling stock content	→	Purchaser doesn't have to create their own content
Instructing a course	→	Students that might not be able to afford college can participate, or the course might be a unique subject not offered anywhere else

When it comes to value and business, the key to understanding how to make a profit by doing virtually anything hinges on five aspects:

1. Creation/transfer of value
2. A want or need
3. An acceptable price
4. Satisfaction
5. Sustainability

To make a profit there has to be some creation or transfer of value, there has to be a want or need for what is being offered, there has to be an acceptable price for the exchanged value, and whatever is being offered in exchange has to satisfy the expectations of both the seller and the purchaser. In order to make a continuous profit so that you can wave goodbye to your day job, you have to embrace the idea of creating these situations continuously so that your PI remains sustainable.

While these aspects may be simplified here in this text, when it comes to generating PI, one must remember that these basic ideals are the cornerstones of guaranteeing successful and long-term income generation.

The Cost of Making Money

I should not have to tell you that making money requires some form of monetary investment. In the introduction, I discussed how some "get rich quick" schemes require payment to get started, but the idea of seed money is different than the "pay to play" requirements that many programs require. In reality, it pretty much costs money to do anything. If you want to flip real estate, you still have to pay for the first house, the materials required to update it, and a listing fee to get the house sold. Developing online courses that people can subscribe to also costs money, as camera equipment might have to be purchased or rented, one might have to rent studio time, and then of course, it might have cost quite a bit of money to learn the skills that will be passed on through the course. Of course, there might be circumstances where money is not an issue, especially if one already has a huge following on social media or a blog, or if someone inherited a house or car that they can easily flip, but for most of us, there is some amount of money that is required to get started. Again, I want to reiterate that this is not a "pay to play" fee where you have to give some company or group money to sell their products, but more of a basic investment in capital or assets that should pay for itself over time.

Generating seed money for PI is almost the same as getting money to start up a business, and should be treated similarly. In any situation where you have to put money on the line, a business plan is the most essential way to not only persuade investors, but also help you understand how likely it will be to generate income. With that being said, a fully-fledged business plan is not necessary for making PI. The main benefit of a business plan is letting investors understand the money-making aspect of their investment. I speak of investors as a separate entity, but with PI, the investor might be you, and you should be able to show, on paper, how the money will be made before you dump a sizeable chunk of money on buying equipment, or purchasing a used car to flip, or taking the time to write a book. The added bonus of coming up with a written plan is that you will not only have a sort of "checklist" you can follow, but you will most likely find other potentials for making money or maximizing your return.

If you absolutely hate the idea of formulating a business plan, at the very least, a SWOT (strengths, weaknesses, opportunities, and threats) analysis should be performed to not only validate your proposed PI function, but also let you know how the most money can be made in the easiest way possible, which will allow you to minimize the costs and effort of making money. I know, this might sound intimidating, confusing, and a little more involved than you thought *passive* income was supposed to be, but I have developed a simplified way of developing a SWOT analysis that will help to make the process painless. I have included examples of how I construct a SWOT analysis for passive income. You can make your own SWOT analysis as detailed as desired.

I want to stress that a business plan or a SWOT analysis is not 100% necessary to make PI. These are just tools that you can use to maximize your success. There are plenty of people who never create a single business plan or perform any analyses, and they still find success. There are many PI activities that do not require much planning, but if you are just starting out and are looking at developing a following/audience or project that you want to convert into PI, it will not hurt to develop a plan that will help to provide some focus to your goals. Even though business planning could technically have its own section in this book, they are primarily used to acquire the seed money that you may need to get your PI project going. Whether you are asking a parent or grandparent for a little bit of startup cash, or even convincing your spouse that the project is worth the time and money, a plan will go a long way in getting you the money you need to start your PI project.

Traditionally, a SWOT analysis is used to determine where a business should align themselves, as it offers a more honest representation of what a business is good at or bad at and how the external environment might affect the business, whether positively or negatively. For the purpose of PI, the SWOT analysis is more personal but less concrete, as you might be more willing to adapt to potential problems than a typical business would adapt to those same issues. For PI, a SWOT analysis allows for an in-depth look at yourself as you figure out how to leverage your time and effort into profitable PI. While I am offering a simplified version, the principles remain the same across all business sizes. Pay attention to the following explanations and examples.

> *INTERNAL:* The STRENGTHS and WEAKNESSES that you can change for yourself, on your own. This might take some work to accomplish in the long run, but you are the ultimate captain of these aspects of your business or PI venture.

>> *Strengths:* What are you good at? Where do you outperform others? What training have you completed? What tools or gear do you already own? These are all questions of the strengths that you can use to determine what PI project is right for you. Fortunately, this type of inward looking also assists in figuring out where to set it up, when to set it up, and how to set it up. Knowing your strengths also helps to validate why you might choose one project over another. For this section, you can list as many strengths as you want, as even the smallest strength might be advantageous in planning for your PI project.

>> *Weaknesses:* Be honest with yourself here. What are you truly not good at? Where can you make room for improvement? Is there something that you know you cannot do? This section requires a

close examination of your own shortcomings as they relate to a potential project.

EXTERNAL: These are the OPPORTUNITIES and THREATS that you must consider that you have no direct control over. These factors can make or break the success of your project, so it is detrimental to be thorough in seeking these out.

> *Opportunities:* If you are selling a used car, living in a rural area, and have few public transportation options this is a great example of an opportunity. Likewise, being a nature photographer living in close proximity to the ocean or a national park is also a strong opportunity. Opportunities are the factors presented by the external environment that you can use to directly benefit or help you with your PI project.

> *Threats:* Opposite of opportunities, threats are factors that the external environment produces that will negatively affect the success of your project. In a sense, you can think of threats as competition or competition inhibitors. If someone else is doing the same thing you are doing, that is a threat to your success. If there is the potential for a barrier to trade, such as a new law that states you cannot sell a particular item, that is a threat.

There are also some abstract threats, such as social media algorithms changing, or affiliate marketers discontinuing their programs. Think of threats as any factor that would make your project more difficult or completely impossible which you have no control over.

VARIABLES FOR SUCCESS: This is the analysis part of a SWOT analysis. After understanding the strengths and opportunities, and figuring out weaknesses and threats, it is important to analyze this information so that you can translate it into variables of success that you can use as a guideline for your PI projects. Recognizing and understanding how your strengths will increase the potential for success will allow you to stay focused on the activities that you know you are good at. Understanding your weaknesses allows for the chance to work on them, or at least avoid those areas where you do not have substantial strength. Even though opportunities and threats are brought forth via the external environment, it is extremely important to be able to recognize each. An opportunity could provide a competitive edge that might minimize a weakness or a threat, while a threat might actually diminish one of your strengths, increase your weaknesses, or ruin an opportunity. When coming up with variables of success, you must understand the core money making function of your PI stream and align it with the information you found in completing a SWOT analysis.

Here are two examples of SWOT analyses I have created to assist you in developing your own. The first one focuses on selling a product (a used car in this case), and the second one is based on building an audience that you can use to sell ad space or post affiliate links. I filled these out as if I were going to begin each project, so the examples pertain to myself, the area I work in, my talents, and my attitude towards each project. Your SWOT analysis should be different. I also confined my worksheet to one page. Yours could, and should, be a great deal longer depending on the complexity of your PI project.

Note: *The italicized sections are what I wrote in for my own PI project by following the aforementioned guideline.*

Example 1:

Selling Used Cars SWOT Analysis
Internal: Strengths and Weaknesses

Strengths

1. *Decent mechanical knowledge*
2. *Know plenty of mechanics that can help when problems arise*
3. *Have access to a garage and tools*
4. *Already have $2,000 of seed money to start*

Weaknesses

1. *Car might have more problems than can be fixed*
2. *Might become too attached to the car*
3. *Could put more money into the car than its worth*
4. *Only have $2,000 to spend*

External: Opportunities and Threats

Opportunities

1. *Two highschools nearby makes selling less expensive cars easier*
2. *Used car dealers in the area price their cars higher than normal*
3. *AWD cars are easily worth $1,500+ in this area regardless of condition*
4. *Facebook Marketplace and Craigslist make selling cars easy in this area*

Threats

1. *Local dealers could drop prices*
2. *Car might not sell as quickly as planned*
3. *Other sellers selling similar cars*
4. *Could lose credibility as a seller if people post negative comments*

Analysis

Variables to Succes

1. *Purchase price must be lower than the acceptable selling price*
2. *If buying a car to fix and flip, the problems must be manageable*
3. *Car must be a desirable make and model*
4. *Money put into fixing the car cannot exceed the minimal selling price*

Example 2:

Developing an Audience SWOT Analysis
Internal: Strenghts and Weaknesses

Strengths
1   *Good with a camera and have camera gear*
2   *I know the surrounding area well, so exclusive content can be created*
3   *Have a decent knowledge of editing software*
4   *Can dedicate a decent amount of time to building an audience each day*

Weaknesses
1   *Not as outgoing as I could be. Somewhat introverted*
2   *Creating consistently good content might be difficult*
3   *Sticking to schedule to create content could be difficult*
4   *Overreliance on social media platforms*

External: Opportunities and Threats

Opportunities
1   *Could collaborate with other content creators*
2   *Can make multiple revenue streams from a single project*
3   *Area has more opportunities for content creation than most*
4   *Local businesses are receptive to content creators working with them*

Threats
1   *Social media platforms make it easy for others creators to do the same thing*
2   *Audience platforms can change without warning*
3   *Trends can change faster than I can adapt*
4   *People might reject my content*

Analysis

Variables to Success
1   *Audience must be satisfied by the content I create*
2   *I have to be happy with the content I create*
3   *I must be able to create new content frequently*
4   *I must be able to create content that is engaging*
5   *Brands must appreciate and seek out my content*

Involvement

Anything that is worth anything takes time and hard work, and this is true of PI. Very few people can say they get PI for free. There is always some form of involvement that goes into the creation of a PI project. Sure, maybe a platinum selling album might provide a pop star with royalties that they can live off of, but it took time for that pop star to learn how to play music, write good songs, promote themselves to the point of being signed by a record label, and then write the hit album that will eventually provide them with that sweet royalty PI. Even stock investors spend time reading the market and researching what companies they want to invest in. When thinking about PI, it is important to remember that it might take time for massive amounts of money to roll in.

The idea of making money without working for it is, for the most part, false. The YouTubers and bloggers you see that make money hand over fist have probably put more time into their projects than they will care to admit. Even though PI seems mostly "hands off" with respect to working a daily 9 to 5, there is still quite a bit of behind the scenes work that goes into PI projects. People who use social media platforms to generate PI have worked hard to curate audiences that are responsive enough to gain the attention of companies and brands that want to buy ad space or provide sponsorships. For those PI earners that sell products, quite a bit of time goes into making money off of those products, such as the time required to search and find flippable products, the time spent adding value to products, and then the final step of selling the product. Those that make money by dropshipping have invested time into creating websites, seeking out products, and then finding ways to sell those products. The instructors that create and sell online courses had to learn the things they were teaching, spend time developing their courses, actually create their courses, and then market them.

I am not adding these examples as a way to scare you off, but to give you an accurate picture of what goes into generating PI. It is true that some PI projects and streams require less involvement than others, but all forms of PI require some form of dedication and involvement.

Touching on those basic value principles I listed earlier, it takes involvement for a PI revenue stream to be sustainable. If the pop star I mentioned earlier does not go on tour, how can they really promote their album? If the social media PI earners do not develop consistent content that pleases their audience, how long can they expect their audience to stick around? In today's world, there are countless distractions that might pull people or brands away from what you are providing them. It takes dedication and involvement to retain that sustainable status.

Of course, I would not bring this idea to light if I did not have some form of solution or way to make the idea of involvement less of a chore. The simplest way is to align your PI project with your hobbies. This is the optimum idea of PI, as you get to make money off of something you enjoy. In many cases, people actually wind up making PI as a means to pay for their hobbies, and the income they generate becomes enough for their hobbies to actually surpass the income from their normal job. Yeah, imagine if you could do your hobby all day and never go to work! The second solution is more difficult, but gets easier as you begin to see results. The second solution involves setting aside time to work on your PI project. This time could consist of monitoring your affiliate links, writing a blog, searching for a used car, perusing a flea market for sellable products, or anything else that keeps your PI project functioning. Allocating time towards your PI project might be difficult, as starting a new habit is never easy, but creating a schedule and sticking to it will not only help maintain PI sustainability, but it will also help you to see other opportunities. The amount of time and the schedule will vary greatly depending on the various different options you might choose to generate PI, but as time goes by and money starts rolling in, you will probably find yourself allocating more and more time to your PI projects.

Even though generating PI does require time and involvement, it requires far less than the active income that most people dedicate 40+ hours of their week chasing after. While you might spend a great amount of time working on your PI stream initially, the end payout might be exponentially larger than if you spent that same amount of time working on an active income stream.

A BRIEF DISCUSSION ABOUT PASSIVE INCOME

Now that I've gone on and on about the principles behind business and what is required of those seeking PI streams, let's discuss how lucrative and fun PI can be. To understand the opportunities that PI can bring forth, we have to understand the ideas behind PI. The major touching points are the differences between passive and active income, exponential growth, and the idea of multiple revenue streams.

Passive Versus Active Income

If you have ever worked for an hourly wage, whether it was at McDonalds or as an hourly paralegal, then you understand the idea of active income. While America's Internal Revenue Service's definitions of active and passive income are overly specific, I will explain these two income types in terms that relate more towards this guide.

Investopedia lists active income as "income for which services have been performed. This includes wages, tips, salaries, commissions and income from businesses in which there is material participation"[1] and lists passive income as "earnings an individual derives from a rental property, limited partnership or other enterprise in which he or she is not actively

---

[1] Kagan, Julia. "Active Income." *Investopedia*, Dotdash, 12 Mar. 2019, www.investopedia.com/terms/a/activeincome.asp.

involved"[2], which are two very fine definitions, however, passive income as we know it has been evolving for some years, and what I say next will most likely contradict Investopedia's definitions.

Having an hourly job, or even a salary-based job, puts a large emphasis on performing specific activities for a set amount of time to earn a set amount of money. You can work extra hours, and the extra money you earn will be proportional to the extra time you spend. In this instance, the limiting factor for your earning potential is a restriction of time. After all, there are only 24 hours in each day. If your hourly wage was $10 an hour, excluding opportunities for over time, the most you could make in a day is $240 if you were psychotic and worked for the full 24 hours. Now, this might change slightly when a salary is involved, but the majority of salaries are determined based on the performance of specific tasks over the course of a set amount of time. While not as confined as an hourly rate of pay, if tasks are not completed or performance is subpar, then salaried employees might be let go. Active income works like an algebraic formula:

One hour of work is equal to the hourly rate.
(1 hour = hourly $)

[2] Chen, James. "Passive Income Definition." *Investopedia*, Dotdash, 9 May 2019, www.investopedia.com/terms/p/passiveincome.asp.

One year of work is equal to a yearly salary.
(1 year = annual $)

These equations can be repeated over and over again with active income as there are few variables, other than a possible negotiation for higher pay, or a promotion. Even then, the only change occurs in the monetary values of each equation.

With passive income, there are no such equations. Of course, one can backtrack and find out how much their hourly rate should be for a PI project, but these rates are fluid, and in some cases, such as affiliate link marketing, while you might see the value of a single link, no two links would have the same value. It would be too difficult to forecast or assign a value to individual links when posting multiple links. How does one place value on a social media audience when social media trends and platforms change so often? Based on Investopedia's definition of passive income, passive income could not exist, as even making money off of rental properties requires some form of participation. People who own rentals still have to ensure they have tenants, make sure tenants follow set rules, make updates to the house, or at the very least, communicate with a property management company. I understand that even this form of participation might be far less than the participation that is required to complete some of the ideas listed later on in this book, but if we were to limit our idea of passive income to the technical definition, then the potential for passive income streams is extremely limited.

For that reason, I have chosen to recognize passive income as any action that generates income without requiring a substantial, ongoing effort, like working a 40-hour work week and has the potential to break out of the algebraic equation demonstrated by active income mentioned previously. Please keep this in mind while reading through this guide.

Essentially, active income is the standard for most jobs where you are limited to what you can make, and every hour spent working yields the same monetary earnings, where passive income requires far less ongoing effort, and due to a lack of limitations such as time, the monetary earnings you can gain are nearly endless.

Exponential Growth

One excellent aspect of developing a PI stream is the fact that a single project can grow exponentially over time with little effort after the initial startup. While exponential growth may not be the same as "going viral", PI projects are fully scalable and increasing potential income does not cost much, nor does it take a ton of effort.

Most successful businesses find ways to use their current brand to facilitate the creation or release of a new brand. Some quick examples of this could be NBC pairing with the International Olympic Committee, Betty Crocker and Hershey's, or even Nike and Apple. These co-branding partnerships provided mutual benefits to each party, and they allowed for each partner to gain an advantage with little extra effort. How much effort would go into NBC developing their own world-renowned competition? How hard would the International Olympic Committee have to work to raise funds and develop their own broadcasting station? Do you see where I'm going with this?

On a smaller scale, outside the world of "business", we see this often with bands that start side projects and use their original band to create and boost the coverage of their side project. Some examples of this are Slipknot and Stone Sour, or even Blur and Gorillaz. On top of this, pop artists are well-known for featuring other artists on their tracks in hopes of reaching new audiences while still creating an appealing collaboration such as Brandon Urie from Panic! At The Disco and Taylor Swift, or the many tracks with seemingly dozens of featured artists on most hip-hop albums. Authors do the same thing: just think about all the Clive Cussler novels that feature a second author.

If you treat your PI project in a similar manner, you can create co-branding amongst your different "partnerships" or PI projects. You can use this same technique to help grow and develop your different PI projects, as each project can act to market and promote your other PI projects.

The growth that comes from this concept is unique to PI. If you were to try to follow this same practice with an active income setup, you would have to dedicate massive amounts of time just to increase your income by a fraction. With PI, you could increase your initial efforts by a fraction and see an exponential increase the revenue you receive from your PI project.

Multiple Revenue Streams

One downside to active income as defined previously is that you are, for the most part, restricted to making one wage from whatever service you provide or activity you perform. In other words, you only get one paycheck from one job. With PI, you can generate multiple revenue streams from a single project.

Just as you can use one PI project to launch a second PI project as mentioned in the previous section, there are many ways that a single PI project could produce multiple revenue streams. While this might not work for every project, if you are creative enough, you will find that most PI projects have more than one option for extra income.

Before I give some examples, remember that the amount of PI you can earn directly relates to the effort you put in the initial setup or planning process. Business gets complicated when you add functions, and this is also true for PI ventures. However, depending on how far you stretch your PI project, you could see quite a bit of added income for very little extra effort.

Example 1: Photo Blogger

If you choose to garner income via affiliated links posted on your photography blog you could also consider selling your images as prints by using a print-on-demand online service. You could also sell your digital photos as stock images. While these two options require very little effort in the way of setup and monitoring, running a successful photo blog can also open the door for selling limited edition prints, a compiled photobook, or even the opportunity to sell time for scheduled photo shoots. These last few items might be more of a side hustle than PI, but you still have the ultimate say on when and how you want to perform these revenue generating functions. Your photo blog PI project that was based on affiliate links could have the potential for five different revenue streams, and I just listed those five off the top of my head. There could be many, many more.

Example 2: Online Courses

Let's say that you want to develop and produce online courses. Many sites offer platforms for these kinds of services, and they are becoming extremely popular. For the sake of this example, let's say you are charging a flat rate for your course. On top of selling access to the course, you could offer one-on-one counseling via webcam, phone, or email for an extra fee, or as a per hour cost. You might think that this requires too much of a time dedication, but you can set it up to where you only allow calls or counseling time on certain days during certain hours, and you could require students to make appointments if they want to participate in these calls. Heck, you could even offer an open conference call on those days. Because you took the time to develop a course, you have already done all the legwork that it takes to compile a book (or eBook). Remember having a required textbook in school where the textbook was not included with the cost of the course? You could follow that same model and sell your book as a supplementary course material. At the very least, you could use your online course to promote a book that you created from the course material. Since you filmed your course, you could also create your own YouTube channel that you can use to sell ad space as well as promote your course and book. These are only a handful of the many options you have to create multiple revenue streams from one PI project.

Since the hardest part of a PI project is the initial creation of the project, it makes the most business sense to try to get as much revenue as you can from a single project rather than starting a new project. Refer back to your SWOT analysis to see where there might be some opportunities to open up more revenue streams. This concept alone could transform a $100 a month idea into a $1,000 a week idea.

PASSIVE INCOME MODELS

Much like typical businesses, there are many different types of PI. While compiling the varying PI projects presented in this book, I found some difficulty in determining a good process for categorizing each project. I came to the conclusion that most projects can be placed in one of three categories. I will go on to explain each category, but keep in mind that these categories can overlap with each project, and these are just basic groups. The three categories, or "models", consist of Freelance/Gigs (FG), Audience Development (AD), and Knowledge Sharing (KS).

Freelance/Gig Model (FG)

The Freelance/Gig model centers on performing a task or creating a product that either ads value or solves a problem. When most people think about freelance work, or gig work, they think of a one-time activity, such as a photo shoot, or playing a concert. Before you get up in arms about the whole active versus passive income debate I brought up earlier in this book, remember the section I dedicated to the discussion of involvement. The reality is that almost every PI stream takes a great amount of effort to set up, but less ongoing effort as the stream grows. Most PI streams start out as a freelance project or gig. The FG model is based on the shift in focus from working for a project rate or hourly rate (active income) to a focus on providing a product that can be sold multiple times (passive income).

This shift in focus still requires effort, as the PI project starts out as an added function of your previous freelance work, but over time you can shift out of earning active income all together. Following the line of photography examples, a photographer that shoots weddings will make active income from either a project rate or hourly rate for each wedding they shoot. However, that single gig could generate quite a bit of PI if the photographer decides to sell some of the images to stock photography websites. As another example, consider a well-known band playing at a concert. Sure they may make quite a bit of money off of ticket sales, but how much money could that band make if they recorded that live set and released it as an album? This is not at all a groundbreaking idea, but how many artists overlook this opportunity?

An important thing to remember about the Freelance/Gig model is that even though the initial activity might be a one time thing, these freelance or gig styled activities can become long term actions, such as purchasing an online business, or utilizing real estate to generate PI. Essentially, these can be grouped under this model since there is no real need to develop an audience or share knowledge in order to generate income through these activities.

Audience Development Model (AD)

The Audience Development model relies heavily on generating enough public interest or a large enough following that you become an influencer. The goal is to get advertisers to see a value in either running ads via your content, or they see a value in sponsoring your content. If you are good enough, maybe you could even promote your own brand or sell your own products. Along these same lines, if you want to try your hand in affiliate marketing, the larger your audience, the higher the chance that your affiliate links will get clicks. Out of all PI projects, those that rely on the AD model probably require the most time and effort to set up and maintain, unless you somehow produce content that goes viral. I don't mean to scare anybody off, but with the ever-changing atmosphere of social media platforms, this type of model can best be described as a labor of love.

While developing an audience takes work, remember that you can use a single audience for multiple PI projects. I should also bring up the idea that you do not have to have a million followers to make money. In 2008, *Wired* magazine's founding executive editor, Kevin Kelly, came up with the "1000 True Fans" concept that focuses on developing lasting relationships with your true fans, rather than focusing on your entire audience.[3] This widely accepted concept is based on the idea that if you can get a thousand people to give you a hundred dollars, you could end up with a six-figure year.

---

[3] Kelly, Kevin. "The Technium: 1,000 True Fans." *Kevin Kelly's Lifestream*,
      KK.org, 4 Mar. 2008, kk.org/thetechnium/1000-true-fans/.

Furthermore, this concept sheds light on the fact that some members of your audience might willingly delve out cash or actively engage with your content, while the vast majority might not give anything. While it does require somewhat of an audience to find potential true fans, whether you are building an audience to sell a product, or to garner engagement through affiliate marketing, keep this concept in mind as you focus on your Audience Development based PI model.

Knowledge Sharing Model (KS)

Many of us have learned quite a bit through our life experiences. For every person that knows something, there are many more who are striving to get a piece of that same knowledge. Many people are willing to pay to gain this knowledge. If you have knowledge that you can share, it is highly likely that there is an audience just waiting to be taught. The Knowledge Sharing model is pretty self-explanatory, as people pay for the knowledge that you want to share, and the exchange is made through the medium you choose.

There are numerous opportunities with this model, as so many people are taking part in web courses, buying eBooks, or even just watching YouTube videos. Given all these media formats, there is quite literally an option for everybody.

If colleges are able to offer full programs via electronic means, there is no reason that the typical PI prospector can't do the same thing. Technology makes sharing, and selling, knowledge extremely easy.

While it's true that you might not be an expert in your field, or even one of the top performers among your circle of coworkers or friends, don't let that idea hinder your hopes. You do not have to be an expert. You don't even have to be good at what you're teaching; you just have to know your content well enough to allow others to understand it. Your viewers/readers, or students (you're a professor now), might see you as an expert if you hit a unique enough niche that has yet to be covered. Whether you create an action specific course, such as how to create an effect in a video editing program, or a more generic guideline, like how to generate passive income, there is a huge audience of knowledge seekers that would rather pay to take an online course or read a book than attend a formal class or college and you can tap into this audience to generate passive income.

Linking Models

As I mentioned at the start of this section, these PI models can overlap. The real triple crown of PI, per se, is utilizing each PI model to achieve your income goals. If you think about the actual functions your PI project requires, it becomes obvious how different functions of a PI project can fall into each model. So how can you link them? Using the photographer example again, not only can you start selling photos from a FG project as prints or stock images, you can also document your process and use platforms like Instagram or YouTube to garner a following that you can use to promote an AD styled model of using affiliate links. Once you have a pretty wide or dedicated audience, it would not be that much more difficult to tap into the KS model by recording how-to's or tip videos, or even writing an eBook detailing your creative process. Some projects might be more difficult to link, but if you are creative in planning, the previously mentioned idea of multiple revenue streams can be even further expanded by utilizing different models.

CHOOSE A STARTING POINT

It might seem daunting to start out, but if you pick the model that suits you best, or has the highest potential for generating PI, then developing these PI streams will come naturally. As you find success in building a stream and spend more time developing it, the opportunities to link models will become apparent, if not blatantly obvious. It does take time to develop the first stream though, so make sure you choose a model that you won't mind spending time developing.

PART 2
The List

THE LIST

The idea of new passive income centers on the concept of finding unique opportunities and converting them into revenue streams. Before delving into the list items, be sure to have a good overall feeling of your current situation. It is hard to maximize income from opportunities when you fail to recognize all of the opportunities you might have. With that being said, don't feel bad if you fail to recognize current opportunities. Opportunities come and go more frequently than we realize, but recognizing those lasting opportunities and capitalizing on them takes some finesse and practice. Sometimes passing up a current opportunity might give you more free time when an even better opportunity comes along. Sometimes a current opportunity might be too good to pass up!

A good idea to keep in mind (or habit to develop) while seeking out opportunities is the idea or habit of thinking more optimistically when considering revenue streams and passive income. This does not mean to grossly over-inflate the money you might make from one opportunity, but being more optimistic about the future opportunities that might stem from your current opportunities will help in setting up dynamic PI revenue streams that have multiple facets. Carrying this optimism forward while thinking in the long term, rather than wholly dwelling on what might make you the most money in the moment will also allow for more future opportunities to provide you with even more potential PI. As you begin to recognize opportunities for their long-term PI worth, you will also realize what opportunities might produce PI revenue streams with exponential earnings or those that might end up costing more than they ever earn. As mentioned before, a major cost could be time, which might be even more frustrating to lose than money. All-in-all, once you are able to recognize opportunity, you will soon find that you can create opportunities for yourself.

With all this being said, the following list is a way of showing the many different opportunities or avenues that exist for those seeking to develop PI revenue streams. Some of the list items do cater to the older style of passive income that consisted of investing in stocks, or renting out real estate, but the list delves a little deeper. Some list items might be one-time gigs that could lead to a more permanent revenue stream, and other items might be lifelong PI activities.

The bottom line is that these list items are potential opportunities that might arise if you are in a given situation. This means that, if you don't like the current opportunities you have, you can work at leveraging your current position to make it line up with more desirable opportunities. This might take more time and effort, but it might well be worth it.

Out of the 350 list items presented, many might seem very alike. This is especially true when discussing ideas in the Audience Development and Knowledge Sharing sections where the list items partly consist of different platforms that could be utilized to garner PI. True, it might be overkill to list every possible print-on-demand shirt company, but if you wanted to start a print-on-demand shirt company, you would likely generate more PI by selling shirts on every possible platform rather than a single, favorite platform. The same could be said of the different online course platforms I list, or even the social media influencing companies I name. Personally, if I spent the time to design a bunch of shirts and develop my own brand, create my own courses, or foster a large audience, I would want to get my content out to as many people and on as many fronts as possible. To me, each one of the many platforms is a new, individual opportunity that should be utilized to maximize PI.

Read through this list with an optimistic, and opportunistic, attitude. Obviously, you might not consider every list item a personal opportunity, but keep in mind that even a single, exceptionally good opportunity might generate enough PI to meet you PI goals.

FREELANCE/GIG PASSIVE INCOME OPPORTUNITIES

Passive Income from Real Estate

Even though real estate might be the most difficult PI stream to break into, it could offer the biggest payoff. I don't need to say it, but there is also quite a bit of risk with real estate, as markets change, the large financial investment requires quite a bit of responsibility, the project might come with plenty of hidden "surprises". Fortunately, with greater risk, there is a substantially larger potential for a huge payoff. If you can get your hands-on real estate, here are some ideas of PI that you can snatch up. Perhaps you already have land or empty industrial buildings that you can upgrade with minimal effort. Here are some examples and ideas of PI for those wanting to play with real estate.

1. Rent out a house.

2. Join a real estate investment group or real estate investment trust (REIT).

3. Rent out individual rooms.

4. Purchase an outdated house, modernize it, then flip it. Seriously, there are dozens of tv shows documenting this.

5. Purchase a foreclosed home and flip it.

6. Purchase a foreclosed home and rent it out.

7. Develop empty lots into new homes.

8. Rent out office space.

9. Rent out studio space.

---

9. An Example: When Greg Johnson originally bought his new ranch home after he retired, he had no need for the industrial sized shop that came with the property. The shop sat empty for a few years, but Johnson came to the realization that there was a substantial market for artists, photographers, and other creatives seeking out studio space. While the industrial shop on his property did need some remodeling, Johnson was able to set up the basic amenities that a studio might need, and started advertising that he had prime studio space for rent. In total, Johnson was able to rent out six different studios under the same roof. Johnson's empty shop allowed him to generate between $1200 and $2000 of PI each month.

---

10. Develop a creator/makerspace lab and rent out stalls.

11. Rent an empty lot as horse or livestock property.

12. Develop an empty lot into storage units.

13. Rent spaces for RV parking.

14. Rent garage space to shade tree mechanics.

15. Rent out extra rooms for AirBnB users.

16. Rent parking spaces to campers/travelers.

17. Rent out garden space.

18. Rent out landscaped areas for weddings and other parties/events.

19. Live close to a college? Rent out rooms to students.

20. Rent out an unused parking space if you live somewhere with a high need for parking.

21. Rent a house out as a group home for special needs kids.

19. An example: Rebecca Springs was renting a house with three other friends while she was attending college. The house she shared with her three friends was within walking distance to a college campus that predominantly catered to commuter students that did not live near campus. After one of her friends graduated and moved out, the friends decided to offer the room up as a pseudo Air BnB where other students could use the room as a study or sleeping space between classes or overnight. The friends agreed on a set price per hour and a set price per night and used the empty room to generate extra cash. Because the room was being rented prior, a portion of the earnings would still have to cover the rent the fourth friend was originally paying, but all the money earned after that contributes to a relatively simple PI revenue stream.

22. An Example: Jeremy Riddel owned a second house that he typically rented to single families on yearly leases. After doing this for about ten years with success, he finally came across a bad renter. When Riddel made a decision to sell his second home instead of renting it, one of his friends persuaded him to look into senior home sharing. Riddel did the research and updated his second home to provide for such tenants, and eventually was able to rent out all three rooms to individual senior citizens. Riddel found that, in addition to more passive income in the form of rental payments, the new tenants were much more pleasant than even the best renters he had in the past.

22. Rent a house out as an elderly foster home.

23. Rent out advertising space on your fence or in your yard.

24. Rent out an empty lot as a place where construction companies can park their heavy equipment.

---

23. An Example: Phil Stevens owned a couple acres bordering the intersection of two county roads. This intersection happened to be the turn off for a busy tourist attraction and tourists would frequently miss the turn. The company running the attraction approached Stevens with the idea of installing a small billboard sign on his lot to point travelers in the right direction. They offered to pay him periodically to "rent" the billboard and Stevens agreed. While Stevens initially built the small structure, the money the company paid him equated to about $60 per month, or $720 per year of consistent PI. Just think what Stevens might be able to do with a bigger billboard and more companies!

Passive Income from Financial Investing

Maybe you already have a chunk of change sitting in a bank account, or you win a large sum of money from a sweepstakes. Maybe you inherited some money from a family member. Regardless, having money makes it much easier to gain more money, especially when it comes to PI. I will refrain from discussing the most obvious forms of investment, like creating a portfolio, but there are some more abstract ideas that could generate some PI as well. Remember, be lucrative and invest intelligently.

25. Invest in cryptocurrency, or better yet, invest in platforms that help mine cryptocurrency.

26. Invest with a robo-advisor such as Betterment, Blooom, or M1 Finance.

27. Invest in dividend stocks.

28. Invest in a high-yield savings account.

29. Invest in money market funds

30. Invest in CD ladders.

31. Invest in annuities.

32. Invest in peer to peer lending (more on this later).

33. Become a silent partner in a business.

34. Buy an established online business using a broker, marketplace, auction, or by contacting existing businesses directly.

Passive Income from Small Start-Ups

Maybe you have a small amount of money to spend, but don't feel like it is enough to create a portfolio, or participate in the other options that were just listed. Perhaps you want to invest in something more tangible that you have more control over. There are many ideas for business start-ups that require very little money, but most do not really fall into the passive category, as start-ups might require a ton of upfront work, as well as continuous effort. The following examples consist of pseudo-passive business ideas that can be managed with an extremely hands-off approach, or with a tighter grip, if desired. These are somewhat traditional business ideas, but I feel that they should be included as PI options on this list.

35. Some Insight: Vending machine businesses have become less popular, but there is still quite a bit of potential to make money from a vending machine business. The trick is placement. Some good places to set up vending machines could be gas stations that have no mini-mart, themed bars, school campuses, business parks, automotive garages, or near government service facilities. The trick is to place vending machines where there is a decent amount of foot traffic and other options aren't present.

35. Vending machine business.

36. ATM business.

37. Party rental business.

38. Storage unit business.

39. Domain name brokering.

---

40. Some Insight: Running a heavy equipment rental business is probably the opposite of what one might call a passive business, but depending on the type of clients you reach out to, a great amount of passive income can be earned from a business like this. In terms of PI, the best option is to serve long term rentals, such as renting a water tender to a logging company for an entire season, or renting a small bulldozer to a construction company for multiple months. There is a large upfront cost for this kind of business, but these kinds of pieces of equipment can bring in a huge amount of PI if rented out to the right customers.

---

40. Heavy equipment rentals.

41. Automotive tool rentals.

42. Film and photography equipment rentals.

43. Recreational vehicle rentals.

---

43. An Example: Chris Prock converts vans into RVs as a hobby, and occasionally sells his projects once they are finished so he can start new projects. Noticing an uptick in tourism in his area, Prock decided to see if he could rent out one of his converted RVs until it would eventually sell. His goal was to have the renters be so happy with the RV that they might decide to purchase it at the end of the rental period. While the first couple people that rented one of his RVs did not buy it, he did make a sizeable amount of PI from the two rentals. On top of this, other people saw the RV for sale and made an offer to buy it. Not only did Prock make PI from renting the RV out, but he also received some free advertising as the renters drove the RV around. While the money made from selling the RV was expected, the supplemental PI from the rentals not only allowed Prock to start his next project, but he was also able to pocket some extra cash.

Passive Income from Purchasing A Business

Many entrepreneurs don't start their own business, but buy someone else's instead. While this might not necessarily work as a PI idea for the typical brick and mortar business, this works extremely well for online businesses. Some online business marketplaces are:

Note: Many of these marketplaces list most of the financial information needed to make solid purchasing decisions when considering the purchase of an existing online business.

44. BizBuySell

45. BusinessesForSale.com

46. Digital Exits

47. Empire Flippers

48. Exchange Marketplace

49. FE International

50. Flippa

51. Freemarket

52. Shopify Exchange

53. Sideprojectors

54. WebsiteBroker.com

Passive Income from Your Established Business

Do you already have an established business or are you an established freelancer? With minimal effort, you can find ways to generate PI to supplement your current revenue. If you have already performed the legwork in setting up work samples, compiled information for a paid project, or have rejected content from a previous client, these are all excellent opportunities for making PI. I use the word gig in this model, since even though some of the ideas I list might not generate constant or sustainable PI, money can still be made with little effort from one-time transactions. Types of businesses vary widely, so the following examples might relate to many different fields and professions. Some of the list ideas presented in this section might require a bit of task finagling in order to make these activities efficient enough to be PI rather than actual gigs.

For business consultants:

55. Create and sell templates and spreadsheets that current and potential clients can purchase and use.

56. Sell examples of previous clients' business plans. Of course, redact sensitive information.

57. Sell marketing information that you have already compiled.

58. Sell potential employee lists to head hunters or small businesses.

For graphic designers:

59. Sell rejected samples as templates for new projects.

60. Develop and sell Photoshop actions, overlays, and other pro-tool specific functions.

61. Sell previous designs as stock designs/templates for other graphic designers to use.

62. Compile a book of previous personal work to sell as a "photo-essay" style coffee table book.

For photographers:

63. Sell stock images on stock image websites.

64. Sell images to newspapers, online news sites, tourist development centers, event organizers, etc..

65. Sell old gear and equipment when you upgrade.

66. Rent out equipment you may not be using.

67. Sell potential client lists to other photographers when you have too much work on your plate.

68. Sell props that you may no longer need or use.

---

63. An Example: Ashley Gelhans is a travel photographer and blogger that already has a decent stream of PI from affiliate links and sponsorships. When Gelhans goes on trips to more scenic locations, such as state parks, she often takes more pictures than the ones she publishes on her site. While some photographers would just delete these pictures, Gelhans squeezes some value out of them. She does this by uploading them to multiple stock image websites where she receives a small payment every time one of her pictures is downloaded or purchased by others. While this amount of PI pales in comparison to her sponsorships, it does provide more money than if she were to just delete the images.

For web developers:

69. Sell website templates to website development sites.

70. Develop and sell plug-ins for blogs such as WordPress or Blogspot.

71. Create website themes and sell them to blogging sites.

72. Develop CMS themes for the blogging and website marketplace.

For music producers/sound engineers:

73. Sell unused songs to vloggers or companies to use as soundtracks or in commercials.

74. Create and sell stock songs.

75. License songs for continued royalties.

76. Create and sell/license stock sounds and sound effects.

77. Compile a sound pack and sell it on sites for other engineers to purchase.

73-77. An Example: Lukas Weebs creates music as a sound engineer. Much of the music he creates ends up either on other's records, or on his own, but the left-over music provides him with a decent PI revenue stream. Weebs uploads stock songs and sound packs to sites like PremiumBeat where he gets royalties each time a song is downloaded and used, as well as a premium when the site buys one of his songs. Weebs also does this without the use of a site, and sells songs to individuals on a commissioned basis. In most cases, a potential buyer hears something they like on Weebs' Soundcloud and asks to either purchase the rights to use it, or pay a use fee. Most of the songs and sound packs that Weebs "sells" were recorded years prior, and the use rights can be sold over and over again with no extra required work from Weebs!

For the mechanically inclined:

78. Buy and sell used cars.

79. Buy cars via lien sales and sell them.

80. Buy or collect lemons and recycle them for cash.

81. Purchase base cars and upgrade them before selling.

82. Sell used OEM parts that still have life via online private selling sites.

83. Offer the service of looking over cars before someone purchases them. This works well if you own an established shop, as it takes little effort and you could charge a decent flat rate for this service.

---

84. An Example: Troy Wellens owns and operates a mechanics shop where his employees perform a slew of automotive repairs. His shop consists of three bays, two of which have lifts. Wellens operates in a city that depends heavily on seasonal tourism. In recent years, Wellens has noticed that in the off season, he only has two bays operating at any given time. While the costs associated with running his shop remain the same throughout the year, he understands that he is losing income when the third bay is empty. Wellens is actively engaged in the classic car community, and when one of his acquaintances lost access to their personal garage, Wellens saw this as an opportunity to generate some PI. Wellens offered to rent out the empty bay for three months so that his acquaintance would be able to finish his restoration project. Wellens was able to convert the potential loss of income stemming from an empty garage bay into PI during the off season with virtually no cost and effort.

---

84. Empty bays in your garage? Rent that space out to budding mechanics and car enthusiasts.

85. Sell old parts to recyclers or scrap metal collectors.

For writers and authors:

86. Sell story outlines you no longer have a use for.

87. Sell developed character profiles you don't plan on using.

88. Sell pre-written testimonials.

For students:

89. Sell class lecture notes.

90. Sell previous tests.

91. Sell previous essays and other coursework.

92. Sell annotated textbooks.

For carpenters:

93. Have a shop full of old supplies? Why not sell them?

94. Sell old tools when you upgrade to new ones.

95. Sell half-finished or unclaimed projects to DIYer's and crafters.

96. Rent out workshop space and tools to budding carpenters and woodworkers.

For tree workers or landscapers:

97. Sell downed trees for firewood.

98. Chip or shred foliage waste and sell to recyclers or lumber mills.

99. Sell foliage waste to gardeners and composters.

100. When replacing a landscape, sell off the removed supplies or use them for another project to save costs.

101. Sell excess materials from previous jobs.

102. Rent out landscape equipment such as tractors, bobcats, etc..

103. Sell old tools when you upgrade to new ones.

---

100. An Example: Jennifer Miller manages a landscape remodeling business. One of her jobs involved the removal of several tall trees that would need to be felled, cut, and slashed. Instead of letting the trees go to waste, she opted to dig the trees up and transfer them to be planted for a different client. While she did not reduce any effort by digging the trees up and transporting them to a different site, she was able to save a chunk of money on the time that would have been spent getting rid of the trees, and she also saved money by not having to buy new trees for the second client. If we think about PI as a means of making money without sacrificing time, this is a prime example!

For those in agriculture:

104. Sell firewood or foliage after clearing an orchard.

105. Sell fill dirt after rotating or changing crops.

106. Rent out grazing land in empty fields or among crops that can handle grazing activity.

107. Have a pond or reservoir with a water supply that provides more water than you need? Consider selling the water to other farmers or ranchers.

104-105. An Example: Claud Hadley owns almond orchards. Whenever he rotates his orchards he must remove the old trees and some of the old soil. This process is typically something Hadley would have to pay for, but years ago, Hadley understood that his trees could produce PI long after they stopped producing almonds. Hadley set up plans with local construction companies and woodcutters to generate income by letting these companies pay to take the soil and trees. In turn, the companies could then process and sell the soils as fill dirt, and woodcutters could chop the trees into firewood that they could sell by the cord. While Hadley could have done this on his own, delegating these activities allows for Hadley to collect an income without sacrificing any of his own time. By maximizing his resources and setting up agreements, Hadley can continue to make money off his trees even after they stop producing.

---

108. Rent out empty barn or stable space for other people's horses or livestock.

109. Sell eggs if you have chickens that produce more than you can eat.

NEW PASSIVE INCOME   A. T. JAMES

110. Sell seedlings if you have more than you can grow.

For those in businesses using a brick and mortar shop:

111. Rent out unused office space to other professionals.

112. Rent out unused storage space to other companies or businesses.

113. Rent out wall space to artists and photographers so they can display and sell their artwork and photos.

114. Have a stage or open space in your business? Rent it out for concerts or plays.

115. Put on a craft fair for local creators and charge booth space.

116. Have empty shelf space? Consider renting out space to vendors.

117. Consider running consignments to both bring in new customers and generate extra income.

PI From Small Investments For Those With Money To Invest:

118. Invest in dividend-paying stocks.

119. Invest in local small businesses.

120. Invest in artists who may need seed money to pay for gallery space or initial printing.

121. Invest in a startup restaurant that may need capital to make their first supplier orders.

122. Invest in a landscape company that may need seed money to purchase new equipment as they expand.

123. Invest in an inventor that is developing a product you believe in.

Peer2Peer Lending

This type of lending is becoming extremely popular. While it is always risky to lend money, peer-2-peer lending is typically done in small enough amounts that the risk is relatively low, but the payback could be extremely high. With most investments, be sure to make a legal contract with clear terms before giving anybody money with the expectation of getting it back.

124. Invest in a product or product line that a company or local business is bringing to market.

125. Invest in DIYer's and crafters.

---

122. An Example: While at the hardware store one day, Greg Navoc overheard a man turning down a potential client due to a lack of equipment and workers. Greg approached the man and asked him about his business. After some discussion, Greg saw the potential of a great PI revenue stream. The man was a budding young landscaper who had some basic pieces of equipment, but not enough equipment to turn his side hustle into a real business. Greg asked for a business card and after much thought, called the man with a proposition. Greg offered the landscaper seed money with the intent that the young man could grow the business with the financial backing of Greg, after which the man could save up and buy Greg out, or continue to give Greg a cut of the profits. While this type of investing might be somewhat small, the small landscaping business could turn into a large scale property management company. The best part about this kind of investment is that these sorts of opportunities are wildly prevalent, and the amount of dedication required to make PI is up to the investor.

---

126. Invest in tourism-based businesses if you observe a tourism boom in a particular area.

127. Invest in advertisement space that you can resell or lease to advertisers, such as newspaper space, billboard space, or even window space.

128. Invest in crowd-funded peer to peer startups.

129. Open a high-yield savings account.

130. Invest in home energy companies, particularly solar and clean energy systems.

AUDIENCE DEVELOPMENT PASSIVE INCOME OPPOR-TUNITIES

Audience Development is based on the concept of utilizing your fans or followers to generate income via a plethora of opportunities. The generation of PI through an audience can come in many forms, but the most basic breakdown of PI streams come from advertiser sponsorships, calls-to-action, or influencer marketing. Someone with a large audience will leverage the use of all three of these options to garner the maximum amount of PI while balancing a constant income stream from their audience. Keep reading for a better explanation of each option.

Sponsorships and Advertising

Companies are continuously following trends to try to either align their products and brands with their potential markets, or promote their current products and brands through platforms and users that are already popular. If you have ever watched a YouTuber, read through a list-based blog, or even checked out a review, chances are you have seen a blurb proclaiming something along the lines of "Sponsored by [insert company here]". Many content creators are paid through sponsors to create these kinds of posts or videos, and this transaction creates a win-win relationship, as the sponsors are able to get their products out there, and the content creator is able to be paid for their content creation. This type of deal is not restricted to the online world, as many sports stars and actors use their publicity to promote their sponsors as well; think about all the times a winning NASCAR driver will say the name of a company in their post-race interview, or the crazy amount of logos behind the podium of a post-game interview. Even though it might be easier to find a sponsor for online content creators, the idea of sponsorships and advertising may be the more difficult of the two aforementioned PI options that having a large audience can generate. With that being said, there are hundreds, if not thousands of companies seeking out representatives that are willing to promote their product. Here are some ideas of the types of content that can be created and used to garner the interest of sponsoring companies and brands.

For YouTubers:

131. Develop a channel that focuses on tech item tutorials or reviews.

132. Develop a channel that focuses on photography.

133. Develop a channel that reviews products that common viewers might want to purchase.

134. Develop a channel based on art tutorials or art reviews.

135. Turn your freelance graphic design gigs into video tutorials that you can upload to your channel.

136. Develop a channel that revolves around a lifestyle.

137. Start a channel that revolves around pets, such as teaching pets tricks.

138. Create a channel that focuses on pet care.

139. Start a channel focusing on food, such as cooking recipes or reviewing restaurants.

140. Develop a music review channel.

141. Start a channel based on one of your hobbies.

142. If you work in a mechanic shop, create car repair tutorials.

143. If you work in a woodshop, document a project's process and turn them into tutorials on a woodworking tutorial channel.

144. Start a makeup tutorial or review channel.

145. If you follow an exercise schedule, film your workouts and upload them as tutorials.

146. If you are big on fitness, develop a channel that does a daily/weekly/monthly workout challenge.

147. If you follow the videogame industry, start a gaming channel where you can do game reviews, playthroughs, or "let's play" styled videos.

148. If you are a DIYer, consider filming how-to's or process videos while you create.

149. If you have willing or easy going friends, a prank channel could be an option.

150. Avid movie viewer? Start a movie review channel.

151. Unboxing videos have become fairly popular. This is a great option if you purchase new items regularly.

152. Start a channel that presents daily quotes and what they mean to you.

153. Travel vlogging is another option to consider if you travel a lot.

154. If you travel frequently, consider making a packing/unpacking vlog channel.

155. Start a tourist attraction review channel if you frequently visit different places.

156. Create a channel that reviews a specific toy line such as LEGO or Nerf.

157. Start a channel chronicling your friends Nerf, airsoft, or paintball battles.

158. If you live in an area with many things to do, consider making a channel focusing on local events, sights, and amusements.

159. Create a channel that gives your point of view or reaction to news events.

160. Thrifting or bargain finding is another good channel idea that could allow you to create good video content. Bonus points if you sell your finds for a profit!

161. Liquidation auctions are becoming extremely popular as unboxing videos. Most of the liquidated goods can be sold for a hefty profit.

157. Some Insight: Large online retailers often get so many returns that it is more cost effective for them to bunch items up in categories and then sell boxes or pallets of random, but categorized goods through liquidation auction sites like directliquidation.com or liquidation.com. Most of the time, the returns are not broken and hardly even used. One could pick up an entire store worth of inventory for a fraction of the selling price. Doing this and running a shop would be outside the confines of PI, but getting these boxes and selling the items to other shop owners could be a PI boon! You could also take items to consignment shops or pawn shops. YouTube channels that unbox these kinds of boxes do extremely well, and selling the goods you unbox could be a secondary benefit!

For bloggers:

Note: *Each option listed in the YouTubers section can be placed in a blog, so I won't bother duplicating those items.*

162. Start a blog that acts as a series of photo-essays.

163. Develop a blog where you can produce short stories.

164. Start a blog that chronicles personal achievements.

165. Create a blog where you post a single picture each day. You can either caption these pictures yourself or allow your audience to come up with their own. Bonus points if your photo is something that is being sold via your affiliate link!

166. Start a blog that disseminates industry specific news and events.

167. Start a blog that helps others. This could be a blog about task keeping, planning, goal setting, or anything that centers around organization.

168. Develop a blog that focuses on financial news and investments.

169. Start a blog that follows grade specific curriculum, such as 5th grade math. Consider offering homework help via the blog (more on this in the Knowledge Sharing section).

Paid Advertising

As mentioned, finding a sponsor for your content may prove to be difficult. An option that is far easier to break into is paid advertising. Paid advertising from the perspective of a content creator or someone with a large audience is the idea of displaying ads alongside your content. There are many different options of generating income from allowing ads to be displayed on your content, and it seems as if new platforms are coming into existence all the time. Here are some paid advertising options that will allow for the generation of PI.

Note: Different paid advertisement systems build up a pay out on a per-view basis, and others are based on a per click basis.

170. You can monetize your YouTube channel to earn money based on a per-view basis.

171. Brid.tv is a platform that can be used to generate a 60% payout of ad revenue.

172. Google AdSense is a platform that offers cutting edge analytics to make the most off of your content.

173. AdRev allows content creators to use more than one platform to generate ad revenue.

Call-to-Action

If you find yourself with a large audience and have already considered, or participated in, sponsorships and paid advertising, there is yet another avenue of PI that could be developed from your audience. Developing a call-to-action may sound like a corny marketing scheme, but leveraging your audience into clicking links, buying products, or even just following a social media account could provide a decent stream of PI. Much like the idea of sponsorships and paid advertisements, there are many options for those wanting to create a call-to-action. The most basic forms revolve around affiliate links, selling a product, or becoming an influencer.

Affiliate Links

Simply put, links on the internet connect different internet resources to each other. These links can be used to expand information, promote products, or even just increase web traffic. Basically, you would post an affiliated link somewhere within your blog post or article (preferably in a place where it makes sense), and every time a reader clicks on the link, you get a piece of the revenue generated from that click through or revenue. An affiliate vendor uses your assigned identity number to track how many clicks your specific link brings in. The use of affiliate links is becoming extremely popular, and to maximize your potential PI you should be diligent in finding the highest paying vendors, or finding vendors with links that would go well with your content. On the flipside, if you are an expert content writer, you can mold your content to fit both specific and generic vendors as well. There are many ebooks and articles written on this type of PI stream, so I will refrain from explaining every aspect of the process, but if you choose to take part in this PI stream, the following is a list of ideas and services that will help you reach your PI goals.

Note: *While blogs and websites are the ideal place to use affiliate links, you can also promote these kinds of links on social media* *and video sharing platforms such as Instagram, Facebook, YouTube, and Vimeo, to name a few.*

174. Rakuten Marketing offers over 2,500 affiliate programs to pick and choose from, which helps if you already have established content.

175. On top of affiliate links, Commission Junction provides both self-managed or company managed options for your affiliate program.

176. Amazon Affiliates has something for everyone, given their huge array of virtually any product imaginable.

177. Google Affiliate Network allows for the easy monetization of links and leads. This does require a Google AdSense account.

178. ShareASale is an affiliate network that offers programs through a host of established blogging platforms. Keep in mind, ShareASale has a minimum payout of $50.

179. Ebates allows you to earn cash back from your purchases as well as their affiliated links. Ebates pays out quarterly.

180. CJ Affiliate has affiliate programs with pretty much any company you can think of. Their minimum payout is $50, but you can select your own payout above that amount.

181. Creative Market caters to those purchasing blog themes and site designs. While this is a smaller niche, the commission for a purchase is 10%.

182. VigLink is an affiliate program that can convert your existing links into affiliate links, which means you can monetize previously written content.

Affiliates Links

Affiliate programs are an excellent and easy way to generate PI. Keep in mind that if generating PI is the primary goal of participating in an affiliate program, you will want to utilize the products that give the best return. Typically, digital products pay the most, but some "hard copy" product payouts aren't too shabby. Remember to write good product reviews to convince your audience to use your affiliate link!

183. Shopify allows users to build e-commerce sites and when you refer customers, you can receive up to the first two months of a new subscribers paid subscription. You can make even more when you refer new customers to the Shopify Plus program.

184. ConvertKit is an email newsletter provider that pays a 30% commission for each subscriber you successfully refer.

185. SkimLinks works like VigLinks, but the revenue split allows for you to receive 75% of the payout. The minimum payout is $10.

186. Booking.com is an excellent affiliate for those that do any kind of travel blogging.

187. Swoop is excellent for those that create content based around food.

188. ClickBank offers tens of thousands of digital products that offer up to a 75% commission.

189. The eBay Partner Network allows you to make a commission when readers click through to items sold on eBay.

Selling a Product

Even though there are many affiliate programs that offer a decent commission, the ultimate commission is the one that allows you to collect all of the revenue. Instead of using your audience to sell someone else's product, consider selling your own. This can be done in a variety of ways, and depending on what you choose to sell, you could either self-fulfill your own product, or use a service to handle virtually everything. The following list provides more detail on individual product niches and ideas, but keep in mind that you will ultimately create a call-to-action with the goal of getting your audience to purchase your product. Since self-fulfilling your own product is more of an active based income stream, I will list the programs and opportunities that lean more towards a passive based model by utilizing a print on demand styled system.

Print on demand systems, or POD, allows you to upload your art or photography directly to the POD website where you can then set the parameters of your product, such as sizes, color options, etc. Most POD sites let you set your own prices, given a minimum, and then they do the rest. All the printing, shipping, and money processing is done through the POD system. While this process is low risk and requires little involvement, it is up to you to market your product. The idea of marketing your product is the reason this PI option is in the Audience Development section. If you already have a large audience of followers or fans, it is pretty simple to start selling your products. Keep in mind that there are many different types of POD systems that cater to many product types. I will do my best to list as many as possible.

Shirts and Apparel:

190. Redbubble

191. Amazon Merch

192. Teespring

193. Society 6

194. Spreadshirt

195. TeePublic

196. Threadless

197. Zazzle

198. Teefury

199. Design By Humans

200. SunFrog

201. Printaura

Art and Photography Products:

202. Fine Art America

203. Zazzle

204. Café Press

205. Printer's Studio

206. CowCow

207. Deviant Art

208. Skreened

209. Saatchi Art

210. Crafted

211. ArtPal

212. Image Kind

213. Zenfolio

Books and Literature (and eBooks!):

214. Amazon Kindle Direct

215. Ingram Spark

216. Blurb

217. Lulu

218. Wordclay

219. CreateSpace

220. Kobo Writing Life

221. Smashwords

222. BookBaby

223. iBooks Author

224. NOOK Press

225. eBookIt

226. Scribd

227. Booktango

228. Trafford

229. iUniverse

Note: *Since the POD site fulfills your customer's orders, you have no control over how the orders are processed and shipped, let alone the quality of the final product the customer receives. Be sure to order test products for yourself to see which POD site works best for you and your customer's expectations.*

Influencer Relations

The idea of influencer relations is a little more abstract than using affiliate links or selling a product. Becoming an influencer is much like becoming sponsored, but is less focused on a brand or product and more focused on developing relationships that will help to build another individuals audience. If you browse Instagram often, you are bound to be familiar with posts published by hub styled accounts that compile and post photos from other users. These kinds of posts utilize the hub's audience to garner an audience for the person whose picture they are reposting. While many hub accounts do this for free, there are many that charge a weekly, daily, or even hourly rate. If you have a large audience, you can charge to promote other's posts as well. Of course, this does not have to be solely based on Instagram, as many people find value in growing audiences on many platforms. The rate you charge is determined on how large of a following you have as well as the niche your followers might fall into. This kind of system creates a win-win for both the hub account and the people paying to be promoted, as the hub account can archive great content without having to create it, and the individual accounts can have a larger reach when the hub account promotes their content.

Various platforms and potential influencer relations:

230. YouTube vloggers promoting each other within their own vlogs (think about challenge videos, reaction videos, or drama/rumor videos).

231. YouTube collaborations among similar videographers.

232. Instagram hub accounts that help to connect individual Instagram users to an exponential amount of fans or even other hub accounts.

233. Instagram hubs that connect models and photographers.

234. Local Instagram accounts that use individual accounts to promote tourism.

235. SnapChat features and account takeovers that allow a user to both promote another account or be promoted by another account.

236. Facebook groups that promote individual pages to a wider, but still specific, audience.

237. Musicians that use Bandcamp or Soundcloud to promote other artists via social media.

238. Selling generic social media accounts that already have a developed audience.

239. Gamers and streamers that use Twitch.tv to promote new video games or newly released downloadable content.

240. Authors utilizing the praise of a more dignified author as a book cover quote. (That's right, influence does not have to be digital!)

As I discussed earlier, making PI from selling influence is much easier if you focus your audience development and influencing sway into a specific niche.

Some niches that are becoming more well-known are:

241. Abandoned Exploration

242. Night Photography

243. Content Creation

244. DIY Projects

245. Art Tutorials

246. Roadside Attractions

247. National Parks

248. Fitness Challenges/Bootcamps

249. 30 Day Challenges

250. Art Support Groups

251. Art Promotion Groups

252. Celebrity Fan Accounts

253. Celebrity Role Playing

254. Local Incident Accounts

255. Video Game Specific Accounts

256. Genre Specific Music

257. Pet Adoration

258. Gardening

259. Action Sports

260. Outdoor Enthusiasts

261. Overland Expedition

262. Makeup Tutorials

263. Business Development

264. Meme Submission Accounts

While the previous lists have hopefully helped to foster an understanding of what influence based PI looks like and a sliver of the niche variety that is out there, the most successful influencers utilize influencer marketing platforms to seek out and facilitate influence-based relationships.

Some of these influencer platforms are:

265. Adly

266. Advowire

267. Blogmint

268. BrandBacker

269. Content BLVD

270. Exposely

271. Famebit

272. Find Your Influence

273. Grapevine Logic

274. Hypr

275. InkyBee

276. InNetwork

277. InstaBrand

278. IZEA

279. Julius

280. Klear

281. Mustr

282. NeoReach

283. Onalytica

284. Revfluence

285. TapInfluence

286. Traackr

287. Upfluence

288. Webfluential

289. Zoomph

Whether you decide to seek out a sponsor, sell ad space, utilize affiliate links, sell your own product, or help influence others with your audience, each one of these PI streams requires an active audience. There are hundreds of books out there that can help you with developing and growing a wide fan base, following, or audience, but remember that you do not have to be well renowned to start utilizing any of the Audience Development based PI streams mentioned here. Let your audience work for you and start making PI based off of your followers today!

KNOWLEDGE SHARING BASED PASSIVE INCOME OPPORTUNTIES

People pay for knowledge and skills. When companies hire accountants, techs, or even managers, they are offering to pay you for the use of your knowledge. Maybe you don't get paid for your knowledge and you actually pay to learn new skills in the form of college classes, online courses, or seminars. Either way, the concept of making PI on sharing your knowledge is nothing new. The idea of making money by sharing your knowledge works much like the other two PI models discussed earlier.

There are many ways to utilize the knowledge sharing model to generate PI, but the main opportunities come in the form of creating online courses, writing educational material, or producing white papers.

Note: *You do not have to be the best, or even an expert in your field in order to develop courses. You just have to be able to convey your knowledge in a way that appeals to potential students. There are many "professionals" teaching courses that might not be considered professionals in their fields, but they still find success in conveying knowledge to an audience.*

Online Courses

Knowledge sharing has become extremely easy due to the use of the internet. What used to be exclusive seminars have become online courses that can be accessed anytime and anywhere. Instead of clearing your schedule, booking a hotel, traveling to an event, and then attending an event, those seeking to learn can now enroll in courses through a variety of sources. The internet has also made it much easier for those who want to develop and sell their own courses, as the upfront costs of putting on a seminar, marketing it, and then actually facilitating physical students have been greatly reduced, if not completely diminished. My argument here is that more time and energy can be put into developing a great platform or course for knowledge sharing all while spending less money. Oh, by the way, you can also recycle courses repeatedly, offer the courses whenever, and you no longer have to rely on filling an auditorium or classroom with students. Everything can be virtual.

Sharing knowledge in the traditional way is admittedly more active than passive as it relates to generating income, but utilizing online platforms and virtual tools enables a PI aspect to knowledge sharing that many successful teachers and instructors are utilizing.

Much like the aforementioned models, there is still work to be done before the PI starts rolling in. Developing courses for an online classroom might take more effort than preparing for a physical seminar, but the extra effort of a virtual classroom allows for the recyclability mentioned a few paragraphs ago. Once a course is developed, you can continue to teach it over and over, and even though I list a plethora of online course systems, this particular activity could be as easy as using Skype, Google Hangouts, or ClickMeeting as a way to offer a "conference-call" styled course that users pay to be a part of. Remember though, to make it even more PI friendly, be sure to record the call so you can upload it again and again. Bottom line: once you develop a class, it can be used over and over, giving the ability to reach exponentially more students. So how does this work?

The physical model of teaching consists of creating a curriculum, developing supporting visual aids, handouts, worksheets, etc., and then facilitating the instruction to an audience in person. The virtual classroom probably consists of the same features, but instead of teaching to a single audience, you could make a video for each lesson or segment of your course, then distribute the videos as students purchase the class. Essentially, when a student enrolls in your course, they are paying for access to existing course materials. As the instructor, all you have to do is sell the course material you have already made. By selling pre-existing material, especially virtual material, the lack of limitations in terms of scaling up to cater to more and more students is obvious. The scalability of this concept has given rise to the mainstream name for these kinds of courses: MOOC, or massive open online courses. There is really no limit to how many students can take the same exact course at the same time. Of course, you may want to tweak the material on a periodical basis, but this can work as a marketing technique to be inclusive to those that may have already found success with your course.

A smart instructor will find ways to create curriculum that builds off of itself. Say you are an expert photographer: you could teach basic design principles in one course such as "How to Take Great Photos", but then you could develop a course teaching more advanced techniques such as "F-Stops: Your Guide to Aperture". As the instructor and course creator, you could offer courses on an individual basis, where students purchase a single course, or you could create packages that students could purchase at one time.

Taking it another step further, you can also sell supplemental material to go along with your courses. If you are a photographer that has developed your own cheat sheets or guides to F-stops, ISO, exposure, and shutter speeds, why not sell that as well? You could develop a worksheet pack to go along with your courses or you could even develop a textbook like ebook (more on this in a bit) that could be sold separately. Rather than just making money by selling a course, you could generate even more PI by selling supplemental materials on the side.

Note: *Bonus points if you reference your supplemental material within your courses!*

While I used photography as my main example, there are courses out their teaching people hundreds of different things. For instance, there are courses teaching pet owners how to train their animals, there are courses teaching people how to draw, hell, there are even courses out there that teach people how to make money through passive income streams!

While the topics covered via online courses are basically endless, here are some of the best sites that you can use to launch your own web classes, courses, or seminars. While some of these platforms offer a framework in which to produce and sell your courses, others are more standalone and only work as a "classroom" in which you can publish and facilitate your course. Even others are plugin-based systems that allow you to sell your course from your own site.

Note: *These platforms vary greatly in what they offer. Some operate as more of a "consulting service" rather than a course system, so be sure to do adequate research to discover which platform will fulfill your needs.*

Opportunities for online courses:

290. Academy of Mine

291. BrainMass

292. Clarity

293. Click4Course

294. ClickMeeting

295. Coggno

296. Cognitive Class

297. Course Cats

298. CourseMerchant

299. Coursera

300. Coursecraft

301. Courseplay

302. Digital Chalk

303. edX

304. Ether

305. FutureLearn

306. Google Hangouts

307. Instructure

308. Iversity

309. Kajabi

310. Kunerango

311. LearnDash

312. LearnWorlds

313. LifterLMS

314. Lynda

315. Maven

316. Openlearning

317. OpenSesame

318. Pathwright

319. Podia

320. PopExpert

321. PrestoExperts

322. ProProfs

323. Ruzuku

E-Courses

Some of the list items I included consist of platforms that deal with consultant-based meetings rather than the traditional "course" style. I included them because you can capitalize on generating PI from these platforms simply by recording the meeting and converting it into more of a "class" format. You can then upload these recordings on other platforms as a course.

324. Saylor

325. Skillshare

326. Skype

327. TalentLMS

328. Teachable

329. Thinkific

330. Udacity

331. Udemy

332. Uscreen

333. UseFedora

334. WizIQ

335. Yondo

336. Zeqr

337. Zippy Courses

Educational Material (eBooks, Guidebooks, Pamphlets, etc.)

Creating educational material, outside of developing a full-fledged web course, is another great way to generate PI via the knowledge sharing model. If you have already developed an online course, then you might want to consider creating supplemental material that can be sold alongside the tuition for the course. Even if you haven't developed an online course, you can still create guidebooks, pamphlets, summaries, or cheat sheet styled materials for existing courses or tests (remember my legal and ethical disclaimers). There are many world-famous courses and tests that have tons of educational materials that were privately developed and sold, seemingly without proper permissions. Needless to say, some of the authors and compilers of the materials not only became quite wealthy, but also became known as experts in their fields. This can be especially true for government-based tests such as state driving tests, contractor licensing tests, or even professional proficiency exams. I am not saying these are work-arounds to get out of taking the tests or courses, but there is a ton of educational material out there that helps people take these courses by providing more, or better information than the course or test might provide.

The typical method of distributing and selling educational material is by publishing and selling books. I already covered POD book printing and eBook options early in this list, so I will refrain from regurgitating that same information. Instead, I will list some other ideas pertaining to the dissemination and selling of educational materials.

Opportunities for PI from educational materials:

338. Write and publish an eBook or physical book detailing unique aspects of a course, test, or subject.

339. Develop an app that might act as a guidebook for any given profession or course. This could be a glossary of terms, list of regulations, simple conversions, or anything related to a specific field. You could sell the app, or receive money from advertisers.

340. Create a website that can function as a database for a specific profession. Make money by selling advertising space.

341. Develop a forum-based website catering to a specific profession, or similar professions, and charge a membership fee.

342. Publish a short handbook that has the bare-bones information needed for a particular course, test, or subject.

343. License out your created curriculum for other educational organizations to use or sell. This can create quite a bit of income from royalties alone, and every time you change your curriculum, you can resell it and relicense it.

344. Create a pocket guide that can work as a cheat sheet for in-the-field use, or a quick reference guide for common information that might be hard to remember (think about financial ratios, command codes, length-distance-are unit conversions, geometric equations, etc.).

White Papers and Grey Literature

One aspect of knowledge sharing that few people consider when seeking opportunities for developing PI streams centers around academic and business-to-business writing. Whether it's an industry report or a recent scientific study, these types of literature are often the most read in a corporate or professional setting. Given the nature of their contents, these are often used as marketing material for companies wanting to offer their business to other businesses, sold as industry updates, or sought out for further reporting and research. Following the value principles mentioned earlier in this book, the alignment of perceived value and a person's willingness to pay for such reports makes these kinds of papers ideal for potential PI streams.

Despite the title of this section, there is a variety of professional papers that can be written as a means to generate a PI stream. While each profession might have a different term for the literature of their field, some common paper types are technical papers, blue papers, green papers, yellow papers, academic articles, and grey literature. If you have a deep knowledge of your field, discover some new method of doing business, answer a unique research question, or can write about any topic a business or organization might want to buy, consider producing these kinds of papers.

Admittedly, getting a PI stream from this kind of activity is extremely difficult, but if you produce papers that are highly valuable, you could net some income, and potentially boost your reputation in your field. I discuss the idea of a "snowball effect" later in this book, and when it comes to selling anything knowledge based, the concepts I mention later will become very relevant.

Another noteworthy consideration is that you might not have to have your paper published in a journal or through another peer-reviewed system at all. There are plenty of white papers, journal articles, and other grey literature being sold under the guise of short books on self-publishing sites like Amazon and Lulu. You can also self-publish and then promote and sell your writings independently. The main purpose to remember is the concept of making money by sharing knowledge through a passive means, so if you do not have a somewhat automated method of selling your papers, this activity might be more active than passive. I feel that the best advice for selling this kind of material focuses on selling it like any other product: ensuring a good website landing page, an automated system of selling (print on demand), and material that has a high value.

Opportunities and Platforms to Sell or Publish Papers:

345. Lulu

346. Amazon

347. Blurb

348. Independently through your own site

349. Independently via traditional selling

350. Sell a use license for others to use your papers

THE LIST IN REVIEW

That concludes the list. Please don't feel overwhelmed by this list. You do not have to try out every single list item I have presented.

While the list is long, it is not one-hundred percent all-inclusive. The list will continue to grow and evolve as new technologies come to market, new industries develop, or new companies offer different marketing platforms. New platforms for conducting business might come into existence, trends will ebb and flow, and customers might want different things. While some of these list items may become obsolete, these new changes will undoubtedly bring about even more opportunities for generating PI.

Now that you understand the concepts, and have a plethora of ideas, how can you get started? What do you need to do to kick off a highly effective and profitable PI project? Part 3 will help guide you on the path that will help kickoff the creation of your very own PI revenue stream.

Note: Any of the aforementioned list items can be researched. I gave a concise overview and examples of the list items that I felt needed to be explained in more detail, but if you find yourself wanting to partake in a list item that you know little about, don't be afraid to spend time researching the ins and outs of a specific idea.

PART 3
Using the List to Make Money

A STEP BY STEP PROCESS

It is incredibly easy to discuss different ways to make money, maximize profit, or establish a revenue stream. Unfortunately, discussion alone will not garner any sizeable chunks of income. You must take action. The knowledge provided in Part 1 is useless unless you know how to utilize it. The ideas I listed out are just pipe-dreams until you start effectively planning your PI project.

So how do you get started?

A hundred-mile journey starts with the first step, and you reach your desired destination by using a map. Here is a rough map of what your PI journey might look like.

Step 1: Assess your current position.
Step 2: Apply a PI model to your situation.
Step 3: Consider 3-4 feasible PI ideas (list items).
Step 4: Decide on the best idea using a SWOT analysis.
Step 5: Start your PI project.
Step 6: Seek out additional PI streams from the project.
Step 7: Find ways to connect to other PI models.
Step 8: Quit Your Day Job?

Step 1: Assess Your Current Position

There is no set, defined starting point, but I would recommend starting from your current situation. Take an introspective look at what you currently do, whether professionally or as a hobby, and align it with one of the models. Consider what you already do for work, or any skills you might have. The idea is to have an easy and efficient transition into PI so that you do not have to put a ton of effort into changing your lifestyle or working long hours to establish a PI base. If you already take pictures as a hobby, it will not be that much more difficult to start a PI project based around photography. If you have never done photography or have no interest in it, obviously you should look at a different PI option or idea unless you are willing to try your hand at something new.

Consider the tangible assets you have at your disposal. If you have camera gear, creating a photography-based PI project would be easier and more cost-effective than if you didn't have camera gear. While gear might be a tangible asset, your photography skills would be an intangible asset that should be considered.

This is like applying for a second job in a way. Consider what you would want to actually work at and use that to sort out what you might or might not enjoy doing.

Step 2: Apply a PI Model to Your Situation

Apply one of the three models to your situation. Is your hobby based on gigs or freelance work? Do you already teach or instruct others? Do you have a decent following? It isn't hard to see how you can define your current situation to fit into one of the three PI models.

I will admit, the FG model is the easiest to break into and the most universal, so I would try to fit that model into whatever you already do, and then start to work your way into the different models.

In selecting a model, keep the idea of being efficient and effective in mind. Select the model that will be the easiest and most immediate to break into. I wrote about using different models, but we will worry about that at a later step. Focus on honing your single PI revenue stream for now.

Step 3: Consider 3-4 Feasible PI Ideas (List Items)

I purposely tried to label each section with industry headers so one could easily comb through the section for the industry or profession in which they already operate and pluck out understandable and relatable ideas. Even though some sections have more than three or four ideas, try to pick the three that seem the most feasible and immediately doable based on your situation or experience.

For instance, as a mechanic, the three items I would choose would be selling OEM parts that still had life, renting out a bay in the garage, and selling old parts for scrap. These three things immediately pop out as being the most low-energy and low-risk.

Step 4: Determine the Best Idea Using a SWOT Analysis

In Step 4, we further break down the three list items we chose by performing a SWOT analysis on each one. This in-depth look at each option will offer more than the cursory glance we took in Step 3. By using the SWOT analysis, we can ask more explicit questions about each aspect of the individual list items. We can then compare the results and determine what the best options are. Sometimes this is obvious, but often, after a SWOT analysis, one finds immediate issues with ideas that might have sounded good on the surface, but in all reality may not work.

For instance, maybe my idea of selling old parts for scrap is unfeasible because the price of metal scrap is too low, or maybe the area is so impacted with scrap metal that clients have to pay to get rid of it. What sounded good initially worked its way into being a non-option.

It might be that all three ideas are great ideas and there are no major differences or challenges to start. If this is the case, take time to use the SWOT analysis to see which potential project falls in line with your goals. Performing a SWOT analysis should help uncover which projects might have major hindrances, which projects might be the most time consuming to start, which projects might have the lowest cost of entry, which projects could bring in more money faster, which projects might have the biggest barriers to success, and the list goes on and on. This portion of picking the best single idea is ultimately based on your own preferences. If you have some seed money, the issue of a cost of entry might not matter to you. If you have a ton of time on your hands, you might not worry about how much time it takes to get a project started.

Step 4 is one of the most crucial steps in developing a passive income stream because it focuses on your personal reality. Because half of the SWOT analysis focuses on potential negatives (weaknesses and threats), it is important to understand how you can use the positives (strengths and opportunities) can be utilized to work towards mitigating or overcoming unforeseen or forecasted issues.

If you know certain threats or weaknesses might exist, maybe the SWOT analysis will help prepare you to overcome these obstacles once they present themselves, or maybe the realization of such problems might push you towards creating a different PI project altogether. An ounce of prevention is worth a pound of cure, so make sure to be thorough in understanding not only all of your weaknesses and threats, but also how you can utilize your strengths and opportunities to plan ahead and strategize how to deal with the weaknesses and threats you may face before you have to face them.

Step 5: Start Your PI Project

Get the ball rolling and start your project. This doesn't have to be anything special like a ribbon cutting ceremony or anything, but you should take note of the day you officially start. This might help for motivating you in the future, and it will certainly help for measuring your success as you continue working on you PI project.

In starting a PI project, practice taking notes on the kinds of activities you do to continue the PI project. Also record your PI project income from time to time. Every good project is backed by good data, so be sure to record the data that you feel is relevant to the continuing success of your PI project. Remember, what can be measured can be managed! This might be as easy as recording audience growth via the amount of people that follow you on a social media platform (hint: platforms have their own analytics programs built in so you don't have to do the legwork!).

Another idea that might help those starting out is to keep money generated from your PI project in a separate bank account. This account will enable you to see exactly how much money is coming from your project, but if you use the account to pay for expenses, it makes it easy to see the true cost of your PI project as well. Furthermore, if you remember the legal and ethical disclaimers at the beginning of the book, having a separate account will make it that much easier to report your earnings when it becomes time to do so. While this idea may seem obvious, the number of sole proprietors and business owners that do not have separate accounts is surprisingly high.

Once your project picks up steam and you have a good grasp on the functions of your PI project, we can start branching off into other PI streams.

Step 6: Seek Out Additional PI Streams from The Project

Once your first PI stream starts producing income, you can start looking at different streams from the same PI project. This is when you can start considering the other two activities that you performed SWOT analysis for. Maybe one of those ideas can be started as a second PI stream. There might be some activities occurring in your initial PI stream that could produce a second stream as well.

After you set up the initial PI revenue stream, setting up other opportunities becomes much simpler. If you already have a system in place to keep track of your activities and how much income you are generating, it isn't hard to replicate it with a second, third, or even fourth income stream. The whole secret is finding a way to create multiple streams without expending much more effort.

The whole concept of passive income centers on the ability to generate money passively, so think about effort efficiency when seeking out multiple revenue streams. Like the first PI stream, the second one should not turn into a full time job. While it may require some work to get started, and additional work periodically, any additional PI streams should be treated like the first.

There are huge benefits in creating multiple streams, especially if they stem from the same initial project. The opportunity of making more income is obvious, but you will also find that the amount of risk incurred becomes more spread out; if one stream falters or fails, you might have others that still flow. You will also be able to fine tune each stream by observing what aspects work and comparing them to the failing aspects of another PI stream. Eventually, you might have a handful of income streams stemming from a single PI project.

Step 7: Find Ways to Connect to Other PI Models

After finding additional PI streams, you can start looking at expanding aspects of your PI project to fit into different PI models.

Even though I have broken PI into three different models, those models are not all-inclusive. A person writing a research paper and developing a YouTube video about that topic to present to their class might fall under the KS model, but it could very easily slide into the FG model if the person decided to sell the academic paper through a journal or if they sell the research to an interested party. It could also slide into the AD model if the person used that same project to develop an audience and eventually sell a product or participate in paid advertising. The whole goal of splitting PI activities into various models is to put forth the idea of "stepping stones". If you start off with a simple expansion of a gig-based FG model, once that is established, you can branch out and try your hand at garnering even more income from the same project, but by using different PI models.

Essentially, a PI project can fit into any model based on how the project is started and continued. However, the real icing on the cake is when a PI project consists of streams that incorporate every PI model.

If you follow the steps up to this point, you might be able to see how the idea of "stepping stones" comes into play. If we labeled the different stepping stones chronologically, this would be the last step in developing your PI project.

Having a PI project with streams that stem from the different models might look something like an artist that accepts freelance work and uses past designs for future designs (FG), runs a YouTube channel where he displays his process and works in progress all while participating in paid advertising (AD), and offers web courses consisting of art tutorials and how-to's on Udemy (KS). The real kicker is that the artist can use the same source material to generate income through all three models. Here's how:

FG: The commissioned piece can be created using old designs or design elements.

AD: The artist can record a time-lapse of his work on the commissioned piece, set it to appealing music, and post it on social media sites.

KS: The artist can also use the commissioned piece to create and record tutorials that can then be uploaded and sold as courses for specific techniques.

As evidenced, it might take a little more work and effort in the way of planning tutorials, setting up cameras, and actually creating the commissioned graphic, but the reach of a single action (creating a graphic) can be expanded three-fold with relatively little effort. By finding different ways to maximize a one-time action, the artist has an opportunity to expand their PI project along multiple PI streams.

Now picture a relatively unknown artist that gets commissioned to do a piece for a famous company, band, or person. Getting such a commission would already be a major boon to the artist's reputation, but the artist should take it a step further and use that same PI stream to branch into other PI models. One would want to maximize their publicity and expand their credibility by utilizing that "endorsement" to the greatest extent possible. You could do this by tapping into every possible PI model as I previously mentioned.

Step 8: Quit Your Day Job?

While this final step is a little tongue-in-cheek, it is totally viable that you might be able to quit your day job after setting up a successful PI project.

Successful PI projects can be continued for as long as they are producing income, or until they revert back into hobbies. While all PI projects are different, they share life cycle similarities.

A PI project can go one of three ways: It can grow, remain stagnant, or dissipate. We'll discuss what to do after a project grows in a second, but first let's discuss stagnation and dissipation.

Stagnation occurs when less effort is being put into a PI project than is required for the project to expand. This does not have to be negative, as many enthusiasts and hobbyists might not enjoy the business side of their hobbies and they opt to continue their hobby as a hobby rather than a PI stream. Maybe a painter enjoys painting for himself rather than accepting commissions. Maybe a photographer would rather focus on creating fine-art portraits than trying to constantly book photoshoots. There is nothing wrong with this idea of going back to the pureness of a real hobby, but in the realm of PI, these projects have become stagnant. These hobbyists might pick up a side gig every once in a while, but they are not trying to expand beyond simple gigs and they won't make the passive income they might have desired.

Dissipation of a project most likely occurs because the person that started the project no longer has an interest in it. Since many PI projects are based off of preexisting conditions, like a current job or hobby, it could be that interest waned, or other jobs or hobbies became more important. If this is the case, the PI project falls to the wayside. This isn't necessarily bad, given the potential low cost of starting a PI project. Even if a PI project creator decided to go after different means of making money, it isn't hard to sell off gear that might have been purchased for the PI project. Unfortunately, the amount of effort and time put into a PI project could far outweigh the cost of equipment, and effort and time are sunk costs that might not be replaced with actual monetary sums.

I saved growth for last because it is the most exciting. Even though the best and most ambitious PI projects can grow into full-fledged businesses, the likelihood of a random PI project becoming the next multi-billion-dollar company is pretty slim. However, PI projects can grow into self-sustaining 'entities' that allow the creator to make supplemental income. In this context, supplemental income can be extremely relative. Is there enough supplemental income to cover the phone bill, utility bills, or maybe even rent? If your supplemental income becomes more than the income you make at work, you could potentially quit your day job and focus on doing what you truly want to do while your PI project brings in the cash you would have had to work a normal 40 hour week to obtain. Once you figure out how to scale up your PI project, it isn't impossible to live quite well without having to worry about clocking in and out of a typical job. The most successful and happy people are those that make enough income to live off of their hobby. If you love doing your job, is it even work?

The ultimate goal of a PI project is to grow the project to a point where it is self-sustaining and produces a desired amount of income. Most investors have a set dollar amount they want to either reach, or receive periodically, when setting up their portfolios. PI projects are no different. While setting up a PI project might not be nearly the same as creating an investment portfolio, once the PI project starts bringing in income, the creator should start considering the monetary goals of the project.

When it comes to developing a PI project, this is the final step. If your project is producing enough income to keep it sustained, or it produces enough income for you to live off of it, I would venture to say that you did pretty well for yourself.

PASSIVE INCOME AS A PATH TO SUCCESS

Some PI project creators and developers might choose not to continue growing their project to the level that I will soon discuss, but I could not write an all-inclusive guidebook to passive income without discussing what might happen after growing and fostering a large PI project. For those that are just starting out, or only have a single PI stream, these ideas may seem like unattainable fantasies, but follow along, and maybe you'll find that the pot of gold at the end of the rainbow does indeed exist.

Eventually you will grow your PI project to a point where it produces benefits that are far greater than the money it provides. These benefits may or may not be obvious, based on your initial goals or attitudes towards developing a PI project. As mentioned prior, a PI project can be as large or as small as needed. For projects that gain major traction, or are ambitiously ground-shaking, the amount of success you achieve could continue to grow exponentially, and I'm not talking about strictly monetary amounts. Much like running a successful small business that eventually either gets noticed and bought by a larger corporation or becomes a larger corporation itself, producing a successful PI project might put you on the radar of some highly successful and highly motivated people. You may even be recognized as a leader in your field. Your idea of success in regards to your PI project may vary, but if you want to go all out and maximize the benefits your PI project has brought forth, there are three potential opportunities that can be realized once your project reaches a certain level. You can be headhunted, you can sell your project, or you can expand your project.

Headhunters

One of the biggest payoffs of developing a successful PI project comes in the form of intangible benefits. While tangible benefits are obvious, such as the money you earn, intangible benefits might not be as apparent at the beginning, but over time, they might become the main driver or asset of your PI project. Intangible benefits are a little more abstract than 'the money you earn', but utilizing your intangible benefits and assets will help you earn even more tangible benefits. Intangible benefits might be considered the fame or notoriety your project receives, especially as it relates to you. Intangible benefits could also be the ability to make more networking connections, attend more conferences, or travel more. These kinds of benefits may be fun or exciting, but they can also turn into excellent assets. You can grow a project much further if you can network more and other possible PI streams might open up when you meet new people in other industries. Fame also has a way of persuading new sponsors to pay you a higher amount and old sponsors to increase their payments. At the very least, if you become more popular, maybe your website will get more clicks and more people will see the paid ads on your site, or they might buy products via your affiliate links.

Successful people coalesce with like-minded individuals. Good managers and CEO's are always looking to bring on new talent. Good companies are constantly seeking people that can bring ideas to fruition. You could be one of these people.

If you can successfully build up a PI project that gains traction, you will probably make a name for yourself in higher circles. Company heads or department managers might begin to look into you and try their hand at getting you to join their teams, and this typically involves handsome salaries or other assorted payouts as offers to get you on board.

When you start making a name for yourself, companies will fall over each other trying to get you to join their teams. These companies might be big, or small, but much like a star athlete picking his team of choice, you may be able to pick and choose where you want to work.

At this point, you can accept or decline these offers. In some cases, you might have quite a bit of leverage depending on how you might fit into the potential positions you are being offered.

If you accept one of these 'dream' jobs, you will have to decide what to do with your PI project. Do you sell the project, do you continue to grow the project, or do you let the project sit how it is? The best part about taking on one of these jobs is that you might be able to continue work on your PI project, or in the least, you can continue to collect money from your PI project.

If you do not accept one of these jobs, you can still use the whole headhunting experience as a unique networking opportunity to further strengthen your intangible assets as they relate to your PI project.

Sell Your Project

This idea is somewhat similar to selling a business. If you find that you can no longer maintain your project, you reached your peak interest in your project, or you want to do other things, maybe consider selling your project. Much like selling a business, there are many options when it comes to selling your PI project. For instance:

1. You could transfer the control of smaller aspects of the PI project and collect a percentage of revenue on a periodic basis, much like being a department manager.

2. You can transfer the control of the entire PI project and collect a percentage of revenue on a periodic basis, as if you were a silent partner.

3. You could sell different aspects of a multi-faceted PI project for cash values.

4. You could sell the whole PI project for a cash value.

Clearly, these four options range in involvement and finesse, but I tried to list them in an order that makes sense according to the idea of maintaining a PI flow or maximizing a profit regardless of which option you choose. Let's consider these options in a little more detail.

1. Transfer Control of Smaller Aspects of Your PI Project

Transferring the control of smaller aspects of you PI project is a good option for those with a little too much on their plate.

Perhaps your project meandered into areas that are profitable, but you have no interest in maintaining. Maybe other aspects of your PI project are far more interesting to you, or follow along with your SWOT analysis better than the segment you might want to discontinue. Don't fear! There are people out there looking to get started on making passive income that would pay a decent amount of cash to hop on board with your project, albeit in a limited sense.

In a way, this is like giving up a small portion of a business. Like a theme park contracting their concession stands to an external company, or an arena contracting out a parking management company, this concept centers around the idea of contracting and subcontracting. While a portion of the business is given up, this reduction of control allows for the project developer to focus on more interesting or pressing project streams.

Giving up this control does not necessarily mean that you are giving up all your profit from that particular stream. Those that may be interested in operating one of your streams would need to pay a premium to be part of the PI project you have already created. This premium could be paid as a recurring payment to the project developer (you), or it could be paid as a percentage of earnings on a periodic basis.

What about a single cash payment for control over a PI stream? We'll discuss this in the third option, but if you want to maintain the breadth of your project and the PI stream you are transferring is closely aligned with the SWOT analysis you originally conducted, opting to retain specific rights to your smaller stream may prove to be more beneficial for the future. Besides, this option still allows for the opportunity of selling off that segment at a later date if you decide to.

2. Transfer Control of the Entire Project

As an extension of the first option, the second option provides an even more hands-off approach to relinquishing your PI project. Rather than picking individual revenue streams to transfer control over to someone else, you might consider transferring control of the whole PI project. If you were to transfer the whole project, much like the first option,

NEW PASSIVE INCOME   A. T. JAMES

you would still be making a sizeable amount of passive income, sans the stress of maintaining any revenue streams.

Surrendering control in this way would most likely consist of the project developer collecting periodic payments or a percentage of income earned from the new controller of the project.

Why would someone want to take over someone else's PI project? Money, probably. The bulk of the energy investment to create and develop a PI project is spent at the very beginning of the project's life, so being able to swoop in on an opportunity that does not have a huge effort requirement is extremely appealing to those seeking easy money. While there is some effort involved to continue PI projects, most of the effort is front loaded. Depending on the complexity of your PI project and the amount of effort invested at the onset, you may be able to ask for a decent percentage of the income after you transfer control.

We see these kinds of deals happen all the time. Think about movie studios paying to use or adapt a specific story or script. Think about toy manufacturers paying for the rights to use a character's name. These kinds of deals are literally going on all the time. These deals also make PI project developers insanely wealthy.

3. Sell Portions of the PI Project for Cash

For many people, their PI project eventually branches out into areas and activities that they might not want to participate in or maintain. If these branches yield PI, then it would be foolish to take an axe to an entire branch due to a lack of interest, especially if it bears fruit in the form of PI. Instead, an alternative would be to sell control of that particular branch to someone that has a high interest in that particular area, or at least someone that might want to maintain it and collect some of their own PI. You could still collect PI from it, albeit slightly less than if you maintained that branch of the project on your own.

In determining which aspects to sell off, or 'transfer', your decision could come from a variety of factors. Perhaps the aspect you want to be rid of is too boring or too difficult. Opportunity costs could also be an issue. Maybe another person is highly interested in taking over a specific aspect of your project and they offer you a decent deal to buy it. Regardless of any of these factors, the most important piece of advice to remember is to consult the SWOT analysis you completed when you first started the PI project. By using the SWOT analysis, you might be more informed when selecting aspects of a PI project that you might want to sell.

4. Sell the Entire PI Project for Cash

Selling the entire project for cash might be the least strategic of the four options listed. The purpose of a PI project is to develop revenue streams that pay out continuously with minor effort or maintenance. Developing a PI project just to sell it is definitely a short-sighted approach to the whole process, but sometimes this type of action makes sense. As an example, if you received a higher cash offer than what your PI project could pay out over a set amount of time, that offer might be something to consider.

Why would anybody offer more money than what you think the PI project could produce? Perhaps the potential buyer sees something in the project that you don't. Maybe the potential buyer already has a PI project that could be complemented by the inclusion of your project (remember exponential growth?). Maybe the potential buyer can use your PI project to capitalize on strengths and opportunities that might be different than yours. Or the opposite may be true and the potential buyer sees your PI project as a way to overcome one of their weaknesses or confront one of their threats.

The opposing side of selling your project for more than it pays out is the option of selling the project for a "loss". I put loss in quotations because it is extremely easy to fall into the trap of the sunk cost fallacy. The sunk cost fallacy is the name for the behavior of letting past decisions of time and monetary investment dictate current decisions. Sunk costs are most easily described as investments that cannot be turned into a return. They are costs that are never reimbursed or recouped. Basically, if you spent a large amount of time and money developing something like a PI project, you might eventually become so attached that you will continue throwing effort into it even though it does not yield a return. As an example, a gambler might keep putting money on the table in the hopes that he can "win back" everything he already gambled away. So how does this relate to "loss"? Well, if you are going to continue to lose money with your project and decide to sell it, you truly might be selling it for less than it might be worth, or at least more than you put into it, but you are also avoiding future sunk costs. Despite technicalities and depending on the situation, this might be considered more of a gain than a loss, at least to a forward thinker.

Selling your entire PI project could bring about a large chunk of change, but what if you truly enjoy the PI project development process and love making that continuous money? Even if you are burnt out with your original PI project, or have to switch away from participating in a specific field, there is another option that can continue to yield generous amounts of PI.

Expand Your PI Project

Expanding your PI project may seem counterintuitive to someone that is trying to get out of the PI game or minimize their involvement in their current PI project, but expanding and realigning your project's goals may be the best way to maximize even greater payouts while minimizing the involvement required.

If you can remember the idea of growing exponentially and using each PI stream as a stepping stone for the next, like we mentioned earlier, then this idea will make perfect sense. Much like using individual streams to hit new streams, a PI project can be expanded and grown exponentially in the same way.

When we discussed the idea of branching out from individual streams we used our SWOT analysis to determine which direction might be the easiest and most efficient to pursue. In the same manner, we can use a SWOT analysis to determine which direction we might take when making large expansions to our current PI project.

Expanding a PI project at this level could probably be considered a paradigm shift, or sea-change shift, but it does not have to be as dramatic as it might appear. For instance, a blogger that develops a successful PI project from running a blog via utilizing all three of the models listed prior could branch out into vastly different areas such as writing and publishing a book, or maybe they could even use the recognition they receive from blogging to delve into other fields or mediums such as creating a podcast. One example of this kind of shift is evident in YouTubers. A YouTuber might gain fame and notoriety by making videos pertaining to one specific genre, such as action sports, pranks, or fail videos, but as trends change, or they develop their channel, those same YouTubers might end up becoming even more well-known for making videos about financial advice, book reviews, or car maintenance. If you didn't follow these YouTubers from the beginning, you might assume that they were two different people.

The real secret is that this single person could have two huge PI projects going on at the same time. If they have blogs, websites, sponsors, and affiliate links set up from when they were creating videos about their first interest, those streams could still produce PI even after the YouTuber switched to a new topic. It may take some maintenance and effort to ensure that those sites are still continuously functional, but the payout would make it worth it. Interests are extremely pliable, and when you find yourself in a position where you might affect the interest of those around you, you can really explore new ideas that might expand your PI project into completely new fields.

While I used YouTube as my prime example, the idea of piggybacking off of a previous success can be applied to almost anything. One famous example is Jared Leto, who not only found success as an actor and director, but also branched out in the music scene with his band, 30 Seconds to Mars, which achieved worldwide fame. Imagine collecting royalties from previous acting roles, and then on top of that, collecting royalties from album sales. Now imagine all the new fans (or customers) you might gain when they realize that they like your movies *and* your music.

Some might say that Jared Leto had a jumpstart from his acting career, but if you develop a successful PI project, and recognize the assets that make up your current PI project, you could have a similar jumpstart as well. Of course, your jumpstart is only limited by how successful your original PI project was, which means the ball is entirely in your court.

The "Snowball" of Success

Regardless of what happens after you craft a successful PI project, it is important to remember that a PI project can be more than just supplemental income. It can become the defining feature of who you are, it can become an asset that you can consider selling, or it can be the kick start you need to boost yourself into different fields, genres, practices, or mediums.

Regardless of what you decide, success works like a snowball. As long as it continues, or keeps rolling, it will get larger and accumulate more mass. If you can remember building snowmen as a kid, you might remember that the bigger the snowball gets, the harder it is to roll, but if you roll it downhill, it rolls much easier, thus becoming larger quicker. Much like that snowball, make sure you aim your "snowball" of success on a path that will work for you rather than against you. You can do this by utilizing the proper planning discussed earlier in this book and by thinking about future PI streams and their potential connections in advance.

PART 4
Before You Go

BEFORE YOU GO: PARTING ADVICE

Now that you have read through this guide, I hope you have a better understanding of the key principles and processes that pertain to new passive income.

We covered quite a bit, but as a quick overview, we touched on the following:

- The legal and ethical aspects of passive income.
- The basic business principles as they apply to passive income.
- The cost of making money.
- The amount of involvement required of a passive income project.
- How passive income differs from active income.
- How passive income can grow exponentially via utilizing multiple revenue streams.
- The different passive income models (FG, AD, and KS).
- We discussed how to use a SWOT analysis to link these models to garner even more passive income.
- I offered up a plethora of ideas that follow the three different models.
- I explain how to use the provided list items to grow your passive income project from a single stream into a multi-project passive income lifestyle.

- I discuss the idea of obtaining tangible and intangible assets from your passive income project and converting these assets into success.

LET'S BE HONEST

At the beginning of this guide, I was upfront about the effort required to craft successful streams of passive income, and I feel that I need to reiterate that same idea here at the end.

It Takes Time

It takes time to develop these projects. While you might make some quick passive income from your current assets, such as renting out a spare room, it still took time to earn the money to purchase that asset in the first place. Musicians blessed with huge royalty payments most likely spent years and years perfecting their musical talents. There is no real shortcut to generating massive amounts of passive income, but the journey does not have to be arduous. The whole premise of this guide is to show you how to utilize your current knowledge, assets, and position to get a good jump start on generating extra cash. I truly apologize if you read this with the intention of making a quick buck without putting forth any effort. The truth is that you need to stay on top of your projects if you want to accumulate the benefits I discuss in Part 3. Yes, you can make a decent amount of pocket change with little-to-no effort, but you must be proactive to gain any sort of wealth.

Find A Balance

If you start this process with the intention of never working again, you might find success. However, it is more likely that you will either burn out before you achieve success, or you become bored with the project you started. There are many people that have a short-lived passion or hobby that they develop into a passive income-based business, only to find they can't stand that particular hobby after a few years. Sure, grudgingly continuing your PI project might be better than clocking in and out at a typical job, but you have to ask yourself if the stress is worth it. Is it? Many people find themselves in the position where the fun of the hobby is overshadowed by the process of making money. I can write a list of hobbyists that come to despise their hobbies later in their careers simply because they find themselves out of balance with the enjoyment of participating in their hobby and the mental stress of maintaining relevance. Take a step back and consider how much you truly enjoy your passions and find a balance.

HAPPY TRAVELS

It is incredibly easy to dream up new ways to make money, but it can be difficult to get started. "A journey of a thousand miles begins with a single step" is a quote often attributed to Confucius, but can be applied to any daunting task. Maybe your goal of seeking passive income has no true end and you just want to make some extra cash, or maybe you have a detailed outline of how you will eventually quit your day job to run a passive income-based business from the comfort of your couch. Regardless, you have to take that first step.

Passive income does not have to be a scary concept. While the majority of passive income is earned through rentals, especially in today's market, it is not difficult to earn passive income from the processes listed and discussed in this guide. It is never too late to start earning passive income, but the sooner you start, the more you can earn.

I hope this guide was eye-opening, intriguing, and informative. Most importantly, I hope this guide will help you to understand the process of developing a passive income project so that you can garner the income you need to break the chains of the typical hourly or salary-based job.

One final note of motivation: If you love doing your work, it won't seem like work at all.

Now go make some passive income!

ABOUT THE AUTHOR

A. T. James writes about business, recreation development, alternative tourism, and evolutionary marketing. A. T. James holds a Master of Business Administration from West Texas A&M University and a Bachelor of Science in Business Administration from California State University, Stanislaus.

A. T. James is a pseudonym of Aaron James, who lives in Tuolumne, California.

www.ingramcontent.com/pod-product-compliance
Lightning Source LLC
Chambersburg PA
CBHW021415210526
45463CB00001B/376